ONE HUNDRED YEARS OF JOURNALISM

ONE HUNDRED YEARS OF JOURNALISM

Social Aspects of the Press

Edited by

Cyril Bainbridge

Foreword by

Lord Goodman, CH

First published 1984

Published by
THE MACMILLAN PRESS LTD
Houndmills, Basingstoke, Hampshire RG21 2XS
and London
Companies and representatives
throughout the world

Typeset by
Wessex Typesetters Ltd
Frome, Somerset

Printed in Great Britain by
The Pitman Press
Bath

British Library Cataloguing in Publication Data
One hundred years of journalism.
1. Journalism—Great Britain—History
I. Bainbridge, Cyril
072   PN5117
ISBN 0–333–38451–2
ISBN 0–333–38452–0 pbk

To Barbara

Contents

Notes on the Contributors

Cyril Bainbridge is Assistant Managing Editor of *The Times*. He began his journalistic career on local newspapers in Yorkshire, where he was born. In 1954 he moved to Fleet Street and spent nine years on the reporting staff of the Press Association. Since 1963 he has been on the editorial staff of *The Times*, where he has been reporter, local government correspondent, feature writer, Deputy News Editor and Managing News Editor. He was President of the Institute of Journalists in 1978. Since 1980 he has been a member of the Press Council. He is also a member of the National Council for the Training of Journalists and the Editorial Advisory Board of the Thomson Foundation.

Sir Terence Beckett has been Director-General of the Confederation of British Industry since 1980. After service in the Army, he began his business career in 1950 as a company trainee with the Ford Motor Co. Ltd, of which he became successively director of the car division, executive director, managing director and chief executive from 1974 to 1980 and chairman from 1976 to 1980. He has been a member of the National Economic Development Council since 1980.

Field-Marshal Sir Edwin Bramall was appointed Chief of the Defence Staff in 1982, before which he was Chief of the General Staff. He served in north-west Europe from 1944 to 1945 and in the Middle East from 1953 to 1958, and had special responsibility for reorganising the Ministry of Defence in 1963 to 1964. He commanded British forces in Hong Kong from 1973 to 1976, and was Commander-in-Chief, UK Land Forces from 1976 to 1978.

Sir Zelman Cowen, Provost of Oriel College, Oxford, since 1982 was appointed chairman of the Press Council in 1983. After a distinguished legal and academic career, he was Governor-General of Australia from 1977 to 1982. He has written and edited numerous legal books, including works on privacy and individual liberty and the law.

Lord Goodman is senior partner of Goodman Derrick and Co., solicitors. He has served on innumerable commissions and inquiries and played a prominent part in discussions on a proposed Press charter. He was chairman of the *Observer* Trust from 1967 to 1976 and the Newspaper Publishers' Association from 1970 to 1975. He was created a life peer in 1965 and appointed Companion of Honour in 1972. He has been Master of University College, Oxford, since 1976.

Sir Kenneth Newman has been Commissioner of the Metropolitan Police since 1982. He served in the Metropolitan Police from 1948 to 1973, reaching the rank of Commander, and the Royal Ulster Constabulary from 1973 to 1979, of which he was Chief Constable from 1976 to 1979. From 1980 to 1982 he was Commandant of the Police Staff College and Inspector of Constabulary.

Lord Scarman has been a Lord of Appeal in Ordinary since 1977. He was a Judge of the High Court in the Probate, Divorce and Admiralty Division (later the Family Division) from 1961 to 1973 and a Lord Justice of Appeal from 1973 to 1977. From 1965 to 1973 he was chairman of the Law Commission, vice-chairman of the Statute Law Committee from 1967 to 1972 and President of the Senate of Inns of Court and Bar from 1976 to 1979. He was created a life peer in 1977 and conducted an inquiry into the racial troubles in Brixton in 1981.

The Rt. Rev. W. J. Westwood, a well-known broadcaster, has been Bishop of Edmonton since 1975 and was vicar of St. Peter Mancroft, Norwich, from 1965 to 1975. He is a member of the General Synod, chairman of the Church of England Committee for Communications and a member of the IBA panel of religious advisers. He was a lay member of the Press Council from 1975 to 1981.

Acknowledgements

Her Majesty Queen Elizabeth the Queen Mother has, in her capacity as Patron of the Orphan Fund for many years, taken a keen interest in the affairs of the Institute of Journalists and I am grateful for Her Majesty's kind message which is incorporated as a preface to this book. My grateful thanks are due to the distinguished contributors for their helpful and immediate response to my requests to them to write on their respective speciality and its relation to the media, and to Lord Goodman for contributing the foreword.

Bob Farmer, who read the draft manuscript, has been most helpful at all times, and two of my colleagues at *The Times* are deserving of my thanks: Pat Davis for many helpful suggestions, and Colin Wilson, Chief Librarian, for providing assistance in my research. Cynric Mytton-Davies' collection of biographies of Past Presidents has been useful as source material and I am also grateful to him for permission to use his small booklet *Journalist Alone* as background on the history of the Freelance Division.

My thanks are also due to my daughter, Mrs Susan O'Sullivan, who typed the manuscript and, finally, to my wife, Barbara, for her interest and understanding throughout the entire project.

C.B.

Preface

I am delighted to learn that the Institute of Journalists is this year celebrating its Centenary.

I offer my warmest congratulations on this important Anniversary and my very sincere good wishes for the years ahead.

ELIZABETH R
Queen Mother
Patron
Institute of Journalists
Orphan Fund

Foreword

I am pleased to have been asked to provide a foreword for this important publication – a book to mark the centenary of the Institute of Journalists, with whom for a number of reasons I have had much to do over recent years while I was the Chairman of the Newspaper Publishers' Association and subsequently engaged in what was melodramatically, though not wholly inaccurately, described as 'the battle for press freedom'.

The IOJ is in many ways a model professional organisation. It provides its members with information on every aspect of their professional activity: it furnishes personal and professional advice; it gives guidance on professional codes and seeks to regulate disputes between its members or its members and their employers. It enjoys a reputation of integrity and decency and the installation of high standards. It has served newspapers well. Above all it performs the crucial duty of negotiating for its members the terms and conditions of their employment: their wage rates; hours of service, and the other essential matters inherent in an employment contract.

It differs in one vital fundamental aspect from the orthodox trade union representing journalists in that membership is wholly and entirely voluntary. A journalist may join if he or she is so minded and if he or she thinks that the benefits that it will bring are commensurate and more than commensurate with the cost of enlistment. It exercises no coercion to recruit members. It recruits them by the simple propaganda of explaining the benefits that would accrue from membership. If a journalist is not satisfied that those benefits are adequate, then no effort is made to twist his or her arm. The importance of this distinction cannot be exaggerated. Had it been a principle employed generally within trade bodies the industrial history of this country might well have taken a very different shape, but that is too big a subject for a short foreword.

The distinguished contributors to this symposium testify to the regard in which the IOJ is held in circles associated with or connected with newspapers. It is not without significance that not a single newspaper proprietor is to be found in the ranks of the contributors. Conclusions can be drawn from this that, alas, are not wholly favourable to the moral courage of these gentlemen. In fact one of the least amiable aspects of recent years has been the speed with which newspaper publishers have bent the knee to the industrial pressure of trade unions. There have been a few honourable exceptions, and in some cases lasting and damaging battles have persisted for many months, but because of the failure of the newspapers to organise themselves together for self-protection against exploitation and against the naked use of coercion, the newspaper industry is in a sorry state.

Publication of this book comes at a timely moment. Newspapers retain their importance in the life of the country. It is a remarkable tribute to the fidelity of their readership that, notwithstanding the vast increase in the quanity and popularity of television, there is no serious suggestion that it is a substitute for a well-informed and truthful newspaper. At the present moment it is not even a substitute for a newspaper lacking these qualities.

Some years ago a crucial battle was fought to seek to prevent the introduction of a closed shop in journalism: that it should be open to journalists who had objections, be they conscientious or economic or simply idiosyncratic, not to have to join a particular union, and the real vice of the matter was that the union that sought to compel their membership could quite capriciously exclude such people from membership or expel them from membership without any legal redress. The battle, in which I played some part, was fought in both Houses of Parliament. The battle is fully described in Miss Nora Beloff's book *Freedom under Foot*. She arrived at the conclusion that we lost the battle because of political naivety. In this she may be right, but my own view is that we lost the battle for the reasons for which battles are normally lost, that our troops were inadequate and, although containing heroic elements, they also contained elements happy to fly from the firing line at the first whiff of grape-shot. That battle reflects credit and more credit on a few heroic figures and, alas, reflects great discredit on a large number of pusillanimous figures.

As a result of the organisation of the press, the sorry situation has arisen in this country where it is a virtual impossibility to establish a new newspaper except at a cost that can be sustained only by immense corporations and plutocrats whose primary qualifications have nothing to do with newspapers but only have to do with their exceptional skill in marshalling wealth. As a result the ownership of newspapers is passing rapidly from the hands of those who feel a deep concern and regard for the maintenance of newspaper traditions and the real purposes they are designed to serve, and into the hands of commercial interests whose primary and natural objective is to increase circulation, often to the disregard of quality and standards.

The IOJ stands for the best end of journalism. That it commands a substantial though very minority membership is a tribute to its qualities to which I have referred. It is an important part of British journalism and I would hope very much that a change of mood may increase its importance and membership over the years. Newspapers are a vital commodity in a well-ordered democracy. The provision of fairly reported and reliable news makes sensible government a possibility. We can in this country still pride ourselves on the fact that the electorate cannot be easily mislead and that however unreliable the reports it has received they do not necessarily have a conclusive effect on the result of elections. One has only to look at other countries to see how important the quality and integrity and truthfulness in newspapers can be if anything approaching true democracy is to be maintained. It is for that reason that I applaud the IOJ; that I wish it well in its centenary year, and hope that its centenary is only a short staging point in its career.

LORD GOODMAN, CH

Introduction

During my Presidency of the Institute of Journalists in 1978 I had the pleasure of travelling to the Hampshire home of the then senior Past President, the late Mr H. A. Taylor, CBE, to present him with his Life Fellowship certificate. An astonishing forty years separated his presidency and mine: years which had seen much change in both the Institute and the profession of journalism.

'Archie' Taylor had begun preparing a history of the Institute's first fifty years but the outbreak of war in 1939 made it necessary to abandon plans for a full-scale official history and his account had to be necessarily brief. The idea for this present volume was born that day in Hampshire: the approaching centenary presented an opportunity to revive the intention of an official history which Taylor never achieved. The idea was supported by a number of friends in the Institute, particularly Mr H. J. Anthony French, who obtained the approval of the Institute Council.

It seemed to me that the occasion merited more than a mere chronological account of events: that it called for a series of authoritative statements on the role of the Press from people prominent in public life, as well as a history of the organisation. The views of the distinguished contributors do not necessarily represent the official policy of the Institute of Journalists, and there may be some who would dispute some of my own conclusions.

So far as the history is concerned, what I have attempted is to set the role and activities of the professional organisation of journalists in the context of the development of newspapers and journalism over the period of a century or more.

It may be questioned why trade unionism has been omitted from the list of contributions. Mr Len Murray, general secretary of the Trades Union Congress, was invited to contribute on the Press and trades unions but declined to do so as the TUC does not recognise the Institute which, of course, is not affiliated to it. It is my regret that the TUC view of the Press has, therefore, gone by default.

C.B.

Part 1

1 Some Observations on the Law and the Freedom of the Press

LORD SCARMAN OBE

The subject of my contribution – the law and freedom of the Press – warrants by way of introduction a brief general comment: by and large, the Press is free and has, in particular, freedom of opportunity under English law. In the light of that observation it is only fair to add that I very much like the American Bill of Rights – and the First Article – and it is consistent with my thinking that there should be in this country a Bill of Rights which ought specifically to declare and protect the freedom of the Press.

What I also believe is needed is a Freedom of Information Act. I have little doubt that the Watergate affair, had it occurred in London, would not have been exposed. The reason for that, however, is not in our laws but in our practice of Government. What is needed much more than any specific removal of restraints from the Press is a Freedom of Information Act, compelling fuller disclosure by Government of what they are doing, what they have done and, to some extent, what their plans are for the future. I feel very strongly that we have not yet analysed correctly where the real mischief is. The mischief is not in our general common law approach to the Press but in the secretive practices of government.

FUTURE DANGER POINTS

The danger points in the future for the law relating to the Press are two: first, the use that can be made by the courts of the weapon of contempt of court – and I think that could fairly be described as

3

having, if it goes too far, a mischievous effect; and, secondly, a very different constraint – and it may be a necessary one – namely the extent to which the development of an effective law on privacy will constrain the Press.

A law on privacy may develop and I think it should, but one has to recognise that it represents a threat to some of the legitimate freedoms of the Press and I believe this to be a difficult area which we have not fully explored. There is a reluctance to provide a legal remedy to protect privacy; and it is an honourable and honest reluctance. I do not think it should stand in the way of the development of a law on privacy but it is a reluctance which we must respect and do what we can to meet the point behind it.

I find it very difficult as a lawyer to draw an understandable line of demarcation between private life and what is in the public interest to be published. For instance, if a judge 'misbehaves' in private life – I do not mean commits unlawful acts but misbehaves in a social sense – I think that is a matter of public interest because it bears directly on his standing in the exercise of his public function. But if my son was to get into trouble of one sort or another, he not being in any way in public life but being the son of a public figure, is there a case for saying that his trouble should be treated as being within the private domain and entitled to protection from publicity? That is an immensely difficult question to answer and I certainly would not give a doctrinaire answer. My inclination is, however painful it be, that, if there is doubt, it should be resolved in favour of freedom of the Press to publish, subject always of course to the laws of defamation.

It will be seen from this how difficult I find this subject, and how very little advanced is my own thinking. Indeed, I would counsel people against moving too fast or too far in developing a law on privacy. I know the Younger Committee reported some years ago and nothing has been done and so, one can say, we are moving neither too far nor too fast – and that is true – but let us not underrate the difficulties. At the end of the day we have got to remain a free, open and tolerant society and if we all live in little secret hideouts there is bound to be a loss of communication and, perhaps, a loss of freedom. Therefore, I am very troubled about law reform in the matter of privacy.

If any developments do come, I think they can come in the world of physical intrusion into other peoples' privacy by the use of the camera, by people who will try and secrete themselves in

private property or get into places where they can see what is
going on. To be told about things by the Press is one thing. To
have people spying out on whoever it may be – the Princess of
Wales or a judge or someone laying by their swimming pool or in
their garden – can I think be stopped without difficulty, and
should be.

As far as television does a journalistic job, I am in favour of
giving them the same protection as I would give the Press, strictly
so called. In so far as they and Press photographers physically
intrude into peoples' privacy I would be in favour of being much
tougher.

INVESTIGATIVE JOURNALISM

As far as investigative journalism and the law is concerned, I
think investigative journalism has proved its social value and I
would not wish to put any curb on it, other than the curbs I have
mentioned on the right of physical privacy, to which I attach great
importance. The other curb I would impose is respect for the
criminal law.

There are matters which really should be left to the police to
investigate and investigative journalists should keep out and if, in
the course of investigation, they come across matters which have a
strong criminal flavour I think their immediate duty – I would not
make this a legal duty for I think this can develop (in the jargon)
by way of a code of practice – is to go to the police and put the facts
in front of them and ask the police whether they think it would be
appropriate for the newspaper investigation to continue or
whether they should put up the shutters. I would not regulate this
by law. Of course, investigative journalism is very much subject to
the risks of contempt of court in some circumstances. They have
got to watch out for what is sub judice and for what might
prejudice a necessary criminal prosecution.

LAW REFORM

Looking at the respective roles of lawyer and journalist in
preserving Press freedom, I think the legal profession have, of
course, an interest in the law and in developing the existing

branches of the law such as defamation, contempt of court, and so forth but where the real development has to take place is not in the world of the practising lawyer but in the world of Parliament, the judges and journalists. Any lawyer who understands his professional duty is going to do the best that he can for his client in any case and, if that means developing with a chance of success a point of law which might appear dangerous to the true interests of the Press, neither he nor his profession is to be blamed for doing it. That is their social job and, of course, lawyers, particularly those who practice in this field, will soon develop their own views about propriety of the law – where it should be reformed and where it should be held back. That comes to them as citizens and they can develop them in the proper way. Their task as a lawyer is faithfulness to their client within the law as it stands.

Of course, the law reformer, the judge and Parliament are critically important in this field. The relationship of the Judges and the Press is a very interesting one and it has developed in a very pragmatic, typically British way, quite unjustifiable in principle but it makes sense. Whatever the law, judges will endeavour in their courts to protect a journalist from questions as to his sources. I did this when I was a divorce judge and, of course, I have done it as a common law judge. Lord Denning has frequently said this is a very necessary judicial attitude and I agree with him. It is quite without any legal basis, except that of commonsense, and the fact that the common law has not ruled on it, that there are no strict precedents, enables the judge to exercise a trained commonsense.

I think that judges are troubled about the quantum of damages awarded against journalists and newspapers in libel and slander actions. This is a very difficult area, particularly if it is a jury award. I think there is something to be said for leaving defamation actions to be tried by a judge alone and never by a judge and jury. My experience of defamation litigation is that it is very difficult: it is technical, it is complicated – it has to be for the number of interests that have to be accommodated. In summing up a defamation action where there are pleas of fair comment, qualified privilege and so forth, a judge undertakes a very difficult task of exposition. Juries understandably and reasonably may be indignant at some publications which are alleged to be libel, but indignation is not a satisfactory basis for the award of damages. A judge can, of course, express public anger and he can reach a view as to whether damages should be exemplary or not but he can do that without losing his *own* temper and he can do it in the knowledge that freedom of the Press is to be recognised in every way, including the moderation of damages when a journalist abuses his freedom.

By and large I would advise journalists not to rush into law reform when they think their interests are in danger. First of all, see what can be done under existing law and by a change of existing practice. If they do want law reform they would be sensible to consult widely and there really is no objection to the Press Council or an individual newspaper or television company putting up a proposal to the Law Commission. The institution is there. It is presided over by a judge – it is independent. Certainly in my time, in the early days of the Law Commission, I welcomed proposals for law reform from the public and I see no reason why that should not be developed.

OFFICIAL SECRETS ACT

Finally, a comment on the much criticised Official Secrets Act. That Act is an anachronism and it ought to go and be replaced. We should draw a distinction between the crime of espionage, which is a threat to the State, and the leak of secret material to the Press which sometimes should not happen and sometimes is absolutely justified. If it should not happen it should not really be the subject of a criminal process at all, but should be dealt with in some other way. I suspect the civil law will take care of it. After all, there is a developed civil law on breaches of confidence; and why should not an employer sack his disloyal employee who communicates his secrets to the Press without his authority?

The Press should not be constrained by criminal law when they come into possession of such information. They can be made subject to the law protecting breach of confidence and they have always got in the background the menace of the defamation action. So, I would confine the Official Secrets Act to what I am sure was its original purpose in 1911 – I would confine it, first by repealing it and then by replacing it with an act designed to deal with the mischief of the disclosure of secrets of importance to national security.

2 Protecting Press and Public

SIR ZELMAN COWEN
Chairman of the Press Council

The assertion of the right to speak, to publish, to know and to make known is one of the great historic claims to liberty. It is made insistently on behalf of the Press and it involves a claim of right to gather as well as to publish what has been gathered and this in turn raises questions, much debated in our times, of the protection of sources of information. A modern American judge has said that the claim to freedom of the Press gives expression to the proposition that without it there can be no free society; freedom of the Press is not an end in itself, but a means to the end of a free society. In one of the great modern cases in which the claim of freedom to publish was considered in the context of the interests of protecting a fair trial, the *Thalidomide* case, Lord Simon of Glaisdale said that:

> the first public interest is that of freedom of discussion in a democratic society. People cannot adequately influence the decisions which affect their lives unless they can be adequately informed on the facts and arguments relevant to the decisions. Much of such fact finding and argumentation necessarily has to be conducted vicariously, the public Press being a principal instrument. This is the justification for investigative and campaign journalism. (House of Lords Judgment, July 1973.)

At the same time, there are limits. Even where, as in the United States, the constitution affirms in the broadest terms that 'Congress shall make no law . . . abridging the freedom of speech or of the Press', it is recognised that this is not without limit and

8

that in the interests of national security, in the assurance of other valid claims to protect important individual and social interests, there are proper constraints upon the freedom of expression and publication. In our British system we do not start with such a constitutional doctrine and we have no special press law; the law which relates to it is, generally speaking, the ordinary law of the land. In law, speech is free except in so far as the law restrains it and therefore the crucial question is what measure of restraint is required in the interests of other individuals and of society. So it is that issues involved in the legal determination of the scope and limits of the freedom of the Press are stated in terms of balance. We can state the point in simple imagery: the right to swing my arm ends at the point where your nose begins. That gives us an approach; it does not give answers to many hard, specific questions.

I have spoken and written about these problems for many years, most recently at the Commonwealth Law Conference at Hong Kong where I led the debate on *The Law and The Press: The Public's Right to Know*. I had undertaken to do that a long time ago; when the Conference took place in September 1983, I was chairman of the United Kingdom Press Council, to which I had come as recently as the beginning of that month. I was surprised, but pleased to be asked to take that important office and in its continuing and demanding work I find myself continually confronted in deciding specific cases involving questions of principle, with problems of balance which, heretofore, I had dealt with more comfortably as a writer and debater unaffected by the need for practical, hard decision.

The constitution of the Press Council, in setting out its objectives, states the first as being to preserve the established freedom of the British Press. It also requires the Council to consider complaints about the conduct of the Press and to deal with such complaints in a practical and appropriate manner. This means that we may seek to conciliate; if that fails we adjudicate upon a complaint and seek to have that adjudication published appropriately. It has been said that there is inconsistency in these objects: that the concerns to protect freedom and assure responsibility do not sit comfortably together. I do not think that this is much of a point: it seems to me that if the Council approaches complaints from the standpoint that the complainant must make out his case within a society which sets a high value on the freedom of the Press – as I think we do – we honour the principles of freedom *and* responsibility or accountability.

I have found it a matter of great interest to observe how the Press Council, in its workings, makes its contribution to defining the role of the Press in a free society. Apart altogether from complaints, it may consider proposed legislation to consider its implications for the freedom of the Press. It does so in the context of legislative proposals to protect privacy, to define the scope of contempt of court, to protect journalists and their material against police search and seizure; it does so, through adjudication of complaints in defining what is and is not permissible. In the area of complaints, there may be cases in which there is an overlap with the law; for example, a complaint may involve defamation of an individual, so that there could be a remedy at law, and in such a case the Council puts the complainant to his election. There are, however, many cases where the objection to Press conduct is not covered by the law, and the argument is essentially an *ethical* one, what is alleged is a breach of ethical standards. Some of our cases concern privacy: that what has been published or what has been done by the Press wrongfully intrudes upon the privacy of the individual without a compensating public interest, that an individual is improperly harassed. In the case of the claim of wrongful intrusion of privacy, there has been a continuing reluctance to provide a remedy at law, for it is said that it is too uncertain, and for this reason would be an unjustifiable constraint upon a free Press. The Press Council has supported this view. It is, however, accepted that the Press Council should adjudicate on complaints of intrusion of privacy, notwithstanding the fact that the criteria on which the Council judges a case involve the very same imprecise elements as a court of law might be called upon to consider. I find this a little puzzling, though I do support a Press Council jurisdiction in these cases. Here, as elsewhere in its adjudication upon complaints, the Press Council does not have a coercive jurisdiction which a court of law possesses.

The Press Council over a wide area proceeds upon the basis that its reasoned adjudications provide an ethical set of principles which should provide guidance to the Press. Even if it lacks a coercive authority, its strength and its credibility depend upon Press acceptance of its rulings and compliance with them, whether it lies in such fields as the intrusion of privacy, misrepresentation or inaccuracy, or in proscribing improper journalistic conduct or 'cheque book' journalism. The Press Council in its complaints jurisdiction is building up a body of rulings and principles which are intended to impose restraints upon the Press, on the principle that it is the obligation of a free but responsible Press to comply with ethical as well as with legal constraints upon its right to publish. It is this which makes it very important for the Press Council to consider its cases in the light of clear principle, and in all cases it must ask the question: is *this* ruling a justifiable and principled restraint upon the freedom of the Press?

One of the frequently expressed criticisms of the Press Council is that it lacks 'teeth'. I have heard and read many times about the 'toothless tiger' and the point is made that the requirements of appropriate publication of adjudications are not always respected; that adjudications are disregarded and that papers ignore or flout rulings. It seems to me that this is a great test of the responsibility of central institutions of a free society: that if we can assure obedience in the fullest spirit to the regime of a non-coercive authority like the Press Council, we shall have shown ourselves responsible elements in a free society. It is a great opportunity and should not be treated cynically. There is also the threat that if a voluntary Press Council fails to secure compliance with its rulings on Press responsibility, that the pressures for the establishment through legislation of a coercive authority possessing legal powers will grow strong and, it may be, irresistible. A Press Council with coercive authority to compel compliance with a wide range of ethical prescriptions will turn those into legal rules and the regime of the law, as it affects the Press, will be substantially extended. I cannot think that a Press in a free society will welcome that; if I am right, I believe that the case for full and ready compliance with a Press Council which is well aware of its own commitment to a free Press is very strong indeed.

3 The Media and Public Order

SIR KENNETH NEWMAN QPM
Commissioner of Police of the Metropolis

Public disorder – in the form of an ugly incident at a football match, violence on a mass 'picket', or a full scale riot – will attract media attention. Indeed people expect, as with everything else that happens in the world, that events of this kind will receive news coverage on television, through radio and in the press as well as considered analysis by commentators, politicians, representatives of the 'authorities' and 'experts'.

All that is part of life. We expect the boxes in the corners of our living rooms and the newspapers that drop onto our door mats to relate the events with impact, accuracy and fairness, and that is perfectly understandable. Disorder is newsworthy and merits media attention.

It follows that the policing of public disorder must take this media interest into account. And if the media has an influence or is at least a factor in the development of events then it is an aspect that police officers must take seriously.

Views about the influence of the media in this context are familiar and various. It is said that the presence of a television crew can inflame an already tense situation and escalate violence. It is also said that media coverage encourages demonstrators to wave, shout and sometimes kick more passionately. It is suggested that a television report of a riot in one place can lead to copy-cat riot in another. Alternatively it is argued that the presence of the media has a calming influence, that potential rioters are inhibited by the idea of their unacceptable behaviour being exposed to the gaze of a censorious world, and that potential troublemakers are not at home waiting to be motivated by television images but are out on the streets providing them.

12

It is easy to offer simplistic explanations. Much thought has been given to the causes of soccer hooliganism, violence on picket lines and full-scale riots. There are no simple answers. If we look at the serious disorder that broke out in Brixton and Toxteth in 1981, we will find a great variety of causes being offered – unemployment, inner city decay, lack of parental control, racism, immigration, economic policy, saturation policing, outside agitators, organised conspiracy and the influence of the media, to name but some.

It may well be that all these factors had a hand in producing a combination of circumstances and factors that led to the 1981 riots. In London, we in the Metropolitan Police – recognising that as the capital city of a parliamentary democracy we attract attention from the world's media and a large number of demonstrations and events with potential public order problems – are keen to analyse causes of trouble in order to act in a way that will prevent rather than inflame trouble. The media undoubtedly has responsibilities too. However, we must all recognise – and perhaps do more to persuade others to realise – that public disorder never occurs solely as a consequence of the action or inaction of the police or press. The community as a whole has responsibility.

For the police I would say that no one should doubt our total acceptance of the fact that the right to public demonstration is a central democratic right. We pass no judgement. We have a duty, on behalf of society, to maintain law and order. On public occasions we seek to communicate and negotiate with organisers to achieve a combination of aims: to allow the organisers of the event optimum expression of their views or make their demonstration within the framework of the law; to ensure that inconvenience to Londoners and visitors to the capital is cut to the minimum; and to see that the least possible commitment of police manpower is achieved within the bounds of what is necessary to keep the peace.

Any public event or demonstration has its publicity element – getting the message across the wider world is almost always one of the aims of the organisers. So the media are being used and should recognise the fact. The police must certainly be aware of that dimension. It operates just as surely, if not as obviously, in the context of public disorder that has no organised beginning but is sparked by an incident which then grows from a combination of circumstances, emotions, motives and misunderstandings. The speed at which events took place in 1981 in widely separated communities must tempt us to conclude that media reports played their part. We must take that seriously.

Commentators have understandably argued that if social constraints on young people were such that limited television coverage was able to undermine them, then the constraints themselves must be at least as much the subject of corporate social attention as the role of the media. Since I have for some time now advocated as part of my policing strategy a multilateral approach to the understanding of crime and disorder, this is a viewpoint with which I can identify.

Nevertheless, a Home Office research study on public disorder published in March 1982 concluded that 'the rapid spread of riots over a period of days in Britain during 1981 provides definite evidence that media reporting was an important element' (*Public Disorder*: Home Office Research Study No 72, 1982). That said, the evidence did not support the view that delays in news reporting of the order of a few hours would have prevented the contagion, and in the United States a moratorium on riot coverage for eight hours achieved little. So we must not be tempted towards simple 'solutions'.

Lord Scarman has pointed out that in multi-ethnic inner city areas of the kind where disorder has occurred, unimaginative, inflexible policing can make greatly worse the tensions which deprivation engenders. Effective policing entails preserving the peace and a sense of public order through the willing co-operation of the law-abiding majority who should be allowed to see that the quality of their lives is, on balance, improved rather than spoiled by the presence of the police. If policing is abrasive and does not take individual or group susceptibilities into account then, however efficient in a mechanical sense, it will not be productive of a harmonious community.

Research suggests that victims of burglary value thoughtful care and attention from the police just as highly as the likelihood of success in finding a culprit. Popular opinion is, therefore, a vital ingredient in policing, and we ignore it at our peril.

This brings me back to the media. Opinion is formed not only by direct experience, but also through hearsay – the Home Office study threw up ample evidence of the harmful effect of rumour during the early stages of a riot – and media contact. It follows that, if reports of an uncritically hostile or sensationalist nature are published, the job of policing becomes that much more difficult.

So what can we do about it? What is there in the police/media relationship that can be enhanced or changed to achieve a direct effect on the level, timing, location or duration of disorder?

Those who will immediately cry censorship in response to this question should look at the work of the Kerner Commission, which investigated American riots in the 1960s. Their conclusion was that the disadvantages far outweighed the likely benefits. There is no doubt, however, that some coverage in particular circumstances can so aggravate delicate situations that special efforts should be made by both media and the police to understand the full implications and exercise sensitive discretion.

The need for this sensitivity has never been more evident than in the context of the events at St. James's Square in London in April 1984. The fact that these events produced tension between police and media perhaps illustrates the point. From the moment of the shooting in the Square – in the presence of television cameras – the Libyan Peoples' Bureau was the centre of attention. The graphic television pictures showing the outrage guaranteed continued media coverage. However, as the Metropolitan Police embarked on a delicate operation to ensure no further bloodshed and a peaceful outcome against a back-drop of international diplomacy, media activity and its potential impact on events became a crucial and sometimes worrying element.

The Libyans inside the Bureau were volatile – that had already been proved with tragic consequences at the start – and were apprehensive and nervous about Press activity and how they would be seen at home. There was constant concern about the Tripoli dimension – events in London and coverage of them were clearly likely to have reciprocal consequences for the 8000 British nationals in Libya. In addition, those inside the Bureau had access to television, radio and telephones and were clearly influenced by what they saw and heard.

All these factors should have inhibited coverage and certainly inhibited the flow of information. One would have expected the sensitivities to be understood but it has to be said that the competitive zeal amongst some of the media to obtain the best story and the best pictures appeared to be the overriding factor at least for part of the time, and caused much anxiety.

Of course, the police and the media co-operate quite happily on a day-to-day basis to mutual benefit. Press, television and radio obtain some of the best of its news coverage from the dramatic events that frequently involve the police. Equally, the police find the media crucially helpful in tracing witnesses and encouraging the passing of useful information. An example of this is the period following the Harrods bomb. There was the possibility of a spate of bombings at that time. Any increase in the number of people in that part of London would have made the task of detecting other devices difficult and would have increased the risk of death and injury. CND had planned a rally and march through the area but police concern at possible congestion was widely publicised and the march cancelled.

Media assistance prior to a major event that has produced disorder in the past has also been worthwhile. In advance of the Notting Hill carnival, publicity is given to police strategy as well as strong crime prevention messages and the disorder of earlier years is now largely avoided. Similarly, following the tragic end to New Year celebrations in Trafalgar Square in 1982, a combination of efficient planning and publicity of routes and facilities ensured a peaceful celebration in 1983.

Perhaps the most outstanding examples of media/police co-operation occur in a case of kidnapping when an agreement, worked out in a meeting at New Scotland Yard with editors in 1975 following the Lesley Whittle case, serves to obviate the dangers of splashing vital information across the front pages. A voluntary news blackout with the aim of reducing risks to the victim has now operated in six kidnap cases.

So, although it can happen that the media and the police have aims in particular situations which can be said to be incompatible, by mutual understanding and sensitivity both can exercise their responsibilities in society without clash. The police should be grateful that press, radio and television offer a system of accountability that can be used to enhance professionalism and quality of service – and can provide, incidentally, a powerful training medium where actions and words can be frozen to our lasting pride or regret. For our part, we hope the media will understand when we appear to restrict or constrain. Both media and police have their responsibilities to the community. Both should understand when the other's aim is paramount. The alliance will be uneasy at times but there is no reason why it should not work.

4 The Press and Industry

SIR TERENCE BECKETT
Director-General of the Confederation of
British Industry

Journalists often complain to me that businessmen will not speak out. I don't agree – and I'll tell you why. It was true ten or fifteen years ago, but in the years since then, I believe the businessman has come out of his corner fighting. Each year, hundreds of CBI members give press, radio and television interviews on issues of vital concern to industry, ensuring that the business case is put across loud and clear, not only to Westminster, Whitehall, the town and county halls, water authorities and others, but also to the public. And by and large business – and the CBI – does enjoy a pretty good press.

But it is essential that the role of wealth-creation is fully understood by everyone. For if business does not thrive, neither will Britain. If we pay ourselves more than we earn, the country will slowly become poorer. If we, as a nation do not make and sell things efficiently, we shall not be able to afford adequate medical services, or roads or schools, or any of the other resources which a modern society needs to flourish.

Businessmen generally are anxious to publicise their activities and their achievements. But there is no room for complacency and self-satisfaction. They should take more initiatives on environmental, health, safety and pollution matters. Inaction here is a short cut to trouble. Look what has happened with asbestos, lead in petrol, and nuclear power. There are vocal groups opposed to them. We must answer them all, clearly, concisely and convincingly. Where their criticisms are justified, we must say so, and take remedial action. Where they are not, we must allay their fears.

Where I suspect some complaints from journalists are justified is in industrial relations. It is no doubt irritating for the reporter seeking a quick quote from the employer during a sudden strike to be met with an ear-splitting silence from the company. It must be equally disconcerting for television producers, seeking to make a programme about the strike and its effects, when they find themselves short of that key ingredient, balance. Hard luck! In a strike situation, there may be very good reasons for silence by the firm. Rule Number One in industrial relations, which I learned very early in my business career, is this: never negotiate through the media.

The shop-floor spokesperson has little to lose. The more extreme the utterances are, the better the workers like it – or so it seemed until two or three years ago, when the tide of industrial relations started to turn. Rank-and-file union members showed they were no longer prepared to walk out of the factory gates to strike on trumped-up pretexts. The hard facts of the recession meant that had they done so, in many cases, their jobs would have gone for good. The British worker is not stupid.

In public relations terms, it is important that the company should seek to keep the initiative during an industrial dispute. A low profile is sometimes – but certainly not always – desirable. There is no golden rule. Telling the media the right facts at the right time can help one's case enormously. One has only to study the tactics of Sir Michael Edwardes when he was at BL to understand that.

I think industry generally gets the Press it deserves. The unfairness creeps in when the media gives free rein to the views of journalists (who are never short of advice to industry on how to handle its affairs and who in many cases are people with no industrial experience). Many could not organise a Press trip round a pottery. I hope I shall be forgiven if the cynic in me says to that kind of journalist, or to his or her employer: physician heal thyself! (and his/her industry's own labour relations).

There is unfairness too, when a paper gets a story wrong in the face of all the facts, and is reluctant to print a reply or correction. That unfairness is compounded when it publishes a correction three weeks later, condensed to about ten lines squeezed into a back inside page on a Saturday morning. This happened a while back after the *Sun* insisted on printing an untrue story about major firms alleged to be resigning from membership of the CBI, which we strenuously denied. None the less it was printed (without our denial).

That kind of incident brings into question the whole of the effectiveness and future of the Press Council. My view is that this body performs a useful function, although I have never sought its help. Its inadequacies – not least the time it takes to swing into action (when it does) – are legion.

But better the Press Council as it is than statutory control. What I find really distasteful is when editors are not big enough to take it on the chin if a Press Council adjudication goes against them. Too often in their papers we have seen a follow-up piece, insisting on the last word, saying why they do not accept the adjudication, and vilifying the Press Council and/or the complainant – often some inoffensive citizen – who is left with no means of redress. Perhaps this is where we could well do with a departure from the convention that the editor's decision is final.

It worries me to see little evidence in Fleet Street today of the pioneering spirit of twenty or so years ago, despite the massive competition which has developed in that time from radio and television. There are too many journalists who are not prepared to go out and dig for the story. It may be part of the malaise which stems from earlier and earlier edition times, which I shall discuss later. Too many reporters are too ready to rely on the handout. Too many regard the CBI, for example, as a neatly packaged organisation, a store-house of information on every subject under the sun. Some time ago, during a rail strike, a journalist asked me how industry was affected. I answered in general terms. The reports we were getting at Centre Point suggested that firms were getting by, despite the difficulties. 'But haven't you done a computer run of your top 100 companies to see how they are getting on?' he persisted. The answer, I need hardly say, was 'No'. It might have helped him a great deal, but it would not have done much for us. I like to help the media as much as I can, but my real answer to this man was: Get off your backside, go out to the regions, and do your own digging.

Then there are those journalists who do themselves no favours, by going about their work, dressed like window-cleaners. They should never forget that they are ambassadors for their papers. It is not all that many years ago that the legendary Arthur Christiansen would lend to any reporter in his office who was not smartly turned out the money to buy a suit. There are some editors who would do well to follow his example today!

Among the national Press, at one end of the spectrum, we have the serious papers, and at the other end, the tabloids, with nothing very much in the middle. Sadly it has been proved – and this must be sickening to any journalist worth his salt – that it is bingo and nudes, not news, that sells the popular newspapers.

It never ceases to amaze me that whenever a title comes up for sale, there is no shortage of hopefuls prepared to pour money into a loss-making venture. What a pity there was no one standing on the sidelines with this kind of enthusiasm in 1960, when the *News Chronicle*, with its long-standing traditions of commonsense and fair-play, went to the wall!

As someone who has spent a lifetime in industry, where the emphasis is on producing the best possible product at the best possible price by the best possible methods, it astounds me that anyone should wish to invest in old technology, and in firms which must be among the world leaders in tolerating restrictive practices. Because of the difficulty of getting new technology into old titles in Fleet Street, it astonishes me that some entrepreneur does not start producing a new technology national newspaper out of, say Retford, Reading or Rugby – or anywhere other than London.

The *Daily Record* in Glasgow – part of the group which publishes the *Daily Mirror* – is technically miles ahead of anything produced in Fleet Street. Right across the country there are some extremely good regional papers, well written and well edited, which have been produced by new technology for years.

Yet Fleet Street is a village of stereotypes – and I don't mean that in a purely mechanical sense. Although it is said to produce national newspapers, they do not always reflect national news. Take a small-scale business conference in Harrogate, or one of the lesser union conferences in Blackpool. These may be big news in the Manchester editions, but often you'll be hard put to find a mention of them 'south of the border' – although the people attending those conferences will have come from all parts of the country.

Self-denigration is another stereotype. Example: the idea that the so-called lazy old British worker helps himself to a fortnight off to recover from the excesses of Christmas and the New Year. It might have been true twenty years ago. But will someone please explain to news editors that in manufacturing industry, management often arranges for people to take part of their annual leave at this time? There is nothing remarkable or disgusting about that. Certainly nothing particularly newsworthy. No one makes a song and dance about it when factories – even some whole towns – close down for a fortnight during the summer. So what's different about Christmas? I sometimes wonder if it is not professional jealousy. Service industries like newspapers try to follow the old showbiz routine – the show must go on – which means some people in the newspaper industry must work when many of us are off duty.

Until the electricians strike of 1955 stopped the Fleet Street presses for a month, newspapers everywhere lived by the precept that the loss of one night's production would be fatal. Yet today, industrial relations in the newspaper industry which so frequently advises other employers how to order their affairs, are in such turmoil that a paper will – and frequently does – miss a night's production at the drop of a line of 12-point.

No one is more seized of the fact that the media can't wait than I am – particularly since I became Director General of the Confederation of British Industry in October 1980. But there are times when the media should accept that industry does not exist purely for its convenience.

In television, I believe some producers are their own worst enemies. I know we live in a quickly changing world, but it really is not good enough to ask a businessman to give up precious time to go to a studio to take part in a programme covering A, B and C, and then, when he gets there to say 'Oh by the way, we've changed the format of the programme. We want to discuss X, Y and Z, not A, B and C.' Or to get him there for a one-to-one interview, and then produce a trade union official and an academic like rabbits out of a hat for a studio discussion. Believe me, things do go wrong occasionally, even with the best-ordered programmes. It happened to me at the time of the last CBI national conference, and I mention it now only because the *Standard* – without asking me – rather unworthily suggested that I ducked the interview.

But if I were producing a newspaper, I would want edition times pushed later, so that I could be turning out something which took into account the competition from radio or television. (Papers will never be able to compete directly, because of the immediacy of the broadcast media.) We now have trains which, thanks to new technology, travel a jolly sight faster than the midnight from Paddington in the days of steam. They should be able to leave later and still arrive in time for papers to be on the breakfast table at their destination. Yet paradoxically edition times get earlier.

The criticism of the media in this article is made in a constructive sense. I hope it wll be accepted as such. We would be living in cloud cuckoo land if we could see nothing wrong in the reporting of the events around us. But having travelled to many parts of the world, I am bound to say that I am left with this conclusion: press, radio and television in Britain are far and away ahead of those in other countries, and I repeat that on the whole the CBI gets fair treatment from the media. However some employers will always find fault with the coverage of their affairs. Not enough coverage of the business scene, they will say. So will the trade unions. Not enough of the union point of view, they will contend. I regard that as essentially healthy. As long as both complain – and keep on complaining – the balance is probably about right. Long may it continue!

5 Reporting Conflict: the Media and the Armed Services

FIELD-MARSHAL SIR EDWIN BRAMALL
Chief of the Defence Staff

The way international conflicts are reported has recently been brought into sharp focus, perhaps more than at any time since the end of the Second World War, even including the war in Vietnam. Our own experiences during the Falklands conflict led to an inquiry by the House of Commons Defence Committee into the way the news media were handled. Only last year the manner in which the American media felt that they had been excluded from the early stages of the United States' operation in Grenada led to a public row.

There are two key issues to be addressed. The first is the role of the media in reporting conflict. The second is their perception and interpretation of that role.

At the end of a talk to the Institute of Public Relations, Henry James, a former Press Secretary in the Prime Minister's office said:

> When there is a conflict between countries operating under different systems of government, a democracy may be at a disadvantage in-so-far as it cannot so readily control the free flow of information and opinion. It is none the less strengthened by genuine consent and the greater credibility of its information at home and abroad.

I agree with that statement. In our society people enjoy certain fundamental freedoms: freedom of speech and freedom of the Press are two of these. But even in a free society there may be matters which it would be improper to release in the interests of national security. However, this should not – and generally does not – imply restrictions on a free flow of information or the expression of opinion. I believe that in a democracy the Armed Services can only work effectively if their operations are acceptable to the people on whose behalf they are undertaken. So, by definition, the Services should seek the support of the media.

Nevertheless, in my view, there is one area where withholding information, at least for a time, may be justified. That is when military operations are impending or actually taking place. Failure to respect an embargo on the release of such information could have the most serious implications for the security of the operation and the lives of those taking part. I am sure no journalist would ever wish to put at risk the lives of our Servicemen. Such a reasonable requirement should be capable of sensible resolution.

If a nation is drawn into conflict the media play a crucial role. Television especially can radically influence the barometer of public opinion. I once heard a very distinguished journalist express the view that the media were not able collectively to present the news without some element of arbitrary distortion. The effect of this on the public cannot be dismissed lightly. When the nation faces crisis the media can make an immediate contribution by their objectivity and calmness and through the recognition of the pressures facing Government and the Services.

Issues of war and peace are not always clear-cut. During a period of international tension, there will be a range of difficult questions affecting whether conflict can be avoided or whether force can be justified in the eyes of the public. The media would certainly wish to take part in the debate. They must take part. But once the nation goes to war, with the support of Parliament, any Government would expect and would welcome the media's help: help in informing public opinion about Government policy, as well as reporting conflict accurately.

Naturally, the media will not accept the Government view without question. If Government statements, however well intentioned, turn out to be false or not supported by events the media will demand to know why. Newspeople have a vital and responsible role to play. Mutual trust and some degree of common interest has to be established. Those managing the crisis should be trained to work with the media. For their part, the media should be finely tuned to the influence they can bring to bear on a national emergency. Only thus can a workable *modus vivendi* be achieved.

It will not be easy to strike the right balance. Control of information, censorship and the effects of modern technology on reporting conflict – these are just some of the problems to be considered before, not after, the shadows of conflict intrude. In my view, if there can be some meeting of minds over these issues then the essential differences between the military and the media may turn out to be positive strengths. The sooner the relative importance of, on the one hand, a military commander seeking restrictions on the release of operational information and, on the other, journalists seeking disclosures, can be established, the better it will be for everyone. We need a bridging operation to ensure that each party understands the imperatives of the other.

By acknowledging that there is a gap and accepting that the aims of the Armed Services and the media are sometimes different – though not essentially incompatible – a start can be made in establishing a positive relationship. The Services and the media need to co-operate constructively about the way in which conflict might be reported in the future. It should not be left to *ad hoc* arrangements.

The media are essential to the preservation of freedom. The Armed Services need their support to maintain public confidence. But once conflict begins we must end it as quickly as possible and with the minimum loss of life. The responsibilities of the media are awesome. They have it in their power to win or to lose battles. And to do this simply by the way they report and interpret events.

6   The Press and the Church

THE RT. REV. W. J. WESTWOOD

Bishop of Peterborough

When I became Rector of Lowestoft in 1957 I went in my first week to visit the mayor of the town and the editor of the *Lowestoft Journal*. At the end of my eight years there had been another seven mayors but the editor was still the same man. More than that, his newspaper sold slightly more copies than there were houses in the town and I realised that my instinct in going to see him had been a sound one.

It would be easy to limit the relationship of the local church and the local newspaper to the reporting of ecclesiastical events with appropriate photographs of vicars, Sunday schools and choirs. All these are important, of course, but I came to learn over those early years that the local paper was the means by which the local community could talk to itself about its life and in that long and developing conversation I wished the Church to have a part. Eighteen years in East Anglia taught me that a good local paper does more than simply listen to the conversation of the community. It can help to create the 'feel' of a place. Every time I return to East Anglia I buy the *Eastern Daily Press* and the sense of the familiar begins to come over me as I read it.

I work in London now. Here it is much harder to establish such a feeling although papers like the *Ham and High* or *The Hendon Times* do frequently fight their way out of the anonymity of metropolitan life, but this is difficult and rare.

Those of us who have valued local papers over the years have a new worry now. So often our papers are part of major groups with headquarters in Fleet Street, our editors are with us for a short time on their way up inside the organisation and our reporters are not just local boys and girls making good but young people serving an apprenticeship which will lead them to the 'nationals' or to television. Above all, we fear that our paper is liable to disappear, overcome by a free sheet where the only conversation in the community then can be between shopkeeper and customer.

I realise, as I write, that my opening paragraphs are an exercise in rural nostalgia but there is also a conversation in the nation carried on in radio and television and in the great national daily and Sunday papers. What I learned in East Anglia has, I believe, something to say about this larger conversation. For here, too, the tone and feel of a nation is not only reflected but can in some way be created. The editor of the local newspaper must choose and select in the midst of reports of council meetings, appearances before the magistrates, funerals and social events. Over the years he or she makes an agenda. Remarkable events and outstanding people will influence adjustments to that agenda but for the most part it stands. It has the advantage that the community can perpetually check the editor and ensure that the agenda is a true one. After all, they may meet the editor at the Rotary Club. After all, the sons and daughters of the sub-editors play in the same school teams as the sons and daughters of readers. After all, the reporters drink at the same pubs as those who keep their paper in the house all through the week and read every page and every paragraph.

The problem for the national newspaper is that the owner, editor and reporters do not have quite the same close links with their readers. Always, it is mediated in one way or another. It is easy for the agenda to be that of the proprietor or editor rather than that of the nation, set by the news itself.

It is easy for the Church to be on the agenda of the local paper for the Church has been there for a long time and is there still. It can, of course, be ignored but that will do injustice to the reality of local life and, in many places, considerably reduce the flow of news.

For the most part, the Church does not seem to be on the agenda of Fleet Street. It is a cliché to say that more go to church on Sunday than go to football matches on Saturday. It is true and yet it is hard to believe it when we read the national papers.

Of course, much of the Church's life and belief cannot be regarded as newsworthy. It lacks that special colour and edge and sparkle that news must possess. However, I have to say that I believe that the Church and its message does not feature on the

agenda for another reason. Not only is the business of the Church
not especially newsworthy but it is also judged not to be
newsworthy. Quite often, then, the Church will appear in the
columns of a newspaper because it impinges upon matters which
are upon the agenda – peace and war, sex, social concern,
foolishness.

Glancing at nineteenth-century newspapers it does seem that
Victorian religion was over-reported – all those sermons and
meetings! Now, I believe that the pendulum has swung too far and
that items of faith and religion, of major concern to masses of
people are now under-reported, to the disadvantage not only of
the Church but also of the newspapers and of the nation they
serve.

The consequence of this is that when matters of religion are
reported, frequently reporters, sub-editors and editors do not
have the 'feel' of a story, often because they have no 'background'
of understanding as, over the years, their newspapers have never
dealt seriously enough with things of religion and Church. There
is a fascinating 'cultural lag'. For example, many who write have a
vision of the Church of England which is really pre-1939. Changes
which have been with us now for thirty years are still described as
'trendy'. The style of worship which marks about 100 of the 130
churches for which I am responsible and has done so for the last
fifteen years is still described as 'way out'. Whenever the Church
seeks to bring the faith of Jesus Christ – Son of Man as well as Son
of God – to bear on the things of ordinary life, in obedience, to the
Lord's second great commandment, then the Church is accused of
some new naive pursuit of politics. Although any church which is
called 'the Church of England' is bound to have some link with
political life and, of course, always has.

This lack of understanding is as much the fault of the Church as
it is of the national newspaper. As an institution we became
beleaguered and defensive. Looking back I have a feeling we lost
our way after the Second World War and as we struggled to find it
again any observation about us in the Press was seen as a criticism
and a slight.

Today we are beginning to get our confidence back. Our
continual decline in numbers has in many places been halted and
in some reversed. More importantly, there is a greater confidence
within the Churches and a greater preparedness to be committed
to a church which people see as their own church. We find more

people concerned with serious issues and anxious to know about the gospel and the faith. Last year over half my confirmation candidates were over twenty.

It would be absurd to talk about religious revival but where I live and work I see signs of serious concern with matters of faith and a readiness among a lot of people to struggle once again with the meaning of religion for their lives. We had got very tired and turned in on ourselves. Today when people talk of a 'new Spring' or use the words of St. Augustine, 'the Easter people', to describe the Church they exaggerate but not much. However I have this uneasy feeling that somehow or another the Church I see is not represented in the pages of the newspaper. I think that I am still on this side of paranoia and I know that my feelings are reflected in many other walks of life where sad and occasionally bitter encounters with the Press have soured peoples' views of the profession of journalism.

May I offer the Institute of Journalists a centenary gift from our own experience. I sometimes think that Fleet Street is like the Church in the 1960s and 1970s (and occasionally today). We pretended to be radical but we offered the same worn-out ways dressed up in awkward modern style. People did not come to us for we did not meet their needs nor touch their hearts.

Perhaps the same thing is happening in Fleet Street. Bingo is no more than the gift-ridden circulation wars of the pre-war years dressed up in modern style. Pretty girls have always been with us and the amount of clothes they wear depends on the custom of the time. Jingoism was popular in 1890 as it is in 1980. Gossip, cruel and kind, has always been easy. However I believe that none of these will deliver the national Press from its current malaise. We found in the Church that only by going back to our roots, only by taking seriously our own failures and inadequacies and only by a re-discovery of our true dignity as a Church were we able to rebuild.

Perhaps the great profession of journalism will be safeguarded for the next hundred years not by bingo, pretty girls, jingoism and gossip but by a re-discovery of 'the dignity of the high calling' which is yours, to hold a true mirror to the nation and to interpret what you see there with courage.

Part II
One Hundred Years of Journalism

Cyril Bainbridge

7 The Formative Years

The Institute of Journalists reaches its centenary at a period of controversy and change in the British newspaper industry – a situation that is a parallel of the time of its inception.

Today it is the advent of so-called new technology that excites equally the enthusiasts and, for different reasons, those who are reluctant to grasp the advantages of the new methods and devices that have revolutionised the production of newspapers elsewhere in the world.

A hundred years or more ago when the first tentative moves were being made to activate an organisation for the benefit of journalists, it was a different sort of revolution that was being experienced: the advent of cheap journalism and the ramifications, among other things, of the early days of what has been loosely called 'the new journalism', and the dilution of earlier professional pride and tradition. Then, it was a sociological rather than a technological revolution that faced the profession of journalism.

The removal of Government levies in the form of stamp, advertising and newspaper duties – what were termed 'taxes on knowledge' – twenty or more years before the Institute was formed had given impetus to journalistic enterprise on a wide scale which manifested itself in a profusion of new newspapers.

In the twenty years from 1851, the number of journals had more than doubled to 1390 newspapers, of which 99 were dailies. By 1880 there were 1986 newspapers and at the turn of the century the figure had reached 2488.

Outbreaks of circulation warfare, particularly in the provinces, were frequent: new publications were started which had a short life-span, often launched deliberately to stifle rival publications. History, it is said, repeats itself: there are similarities in that historic situation and the recent competition brought about by the widespread introduction of free newspapers.

Weekly newspapers at that time were frequently launched with little capital and as an adjunct of a general printing or some other business. There was, no doubt because of the advertising potential, an odd affinity between purveyors of pills and local newspapers: many instances are recorded of chemists and their families launching newspapers – a rather droll mixture of chemistry and culture.

Undoubtedly there was an irresponsible element whose motives and methods were open to suspicion and scrutiny; 'greengrocer' and 'huckstering' proprietors were contemporary derogatory descriptions. But many of the new newspapers were more soundly based financially and more responsible in their approach and coverage of news. They survived and many are still in existence.

The creation of new newspapers on this scale led to a great demand for people with which to staff them. The style of journalism of the period was such that either a remarkable memory or a knowledge of one of the many systems of shorthand was necessary to meet the demands for the long verbatim reports of political speeches which were then a staple of newspaper content.

A shorthand wave swept over journalism bringing into it, as a writer in *The Journalist and Newspaper Proprietor* stated, 'many good men but flooding it with a host of the wholly uneducated and the half-instructed'.

The 'shorthand wave' was not the only evil the traditional journalist had to contend with. The same correspondent added:

Small capitalists of all trades who know nothing of Press traditions, perceived that newspapers worked on grabbing lines were a good 'lay' and they ran newspapers. The people who knew a little shorthand and still less of English grammar were the lifebuoys of these gentry and between the two the trained journalist had a hard time of it.

It was against this scenario that the first cautious steps were taken to remedy the disadvantages journalists suffered through having no corporate voice or organisation to represent them.

Much of the force behind the moves came from the north of England and Manchester in particular. No specific matter appears to have sparked off the initiative but the occasion was provided by the gathering of 'a goodly number' of journalists in

York in mid-July 1883 to report the Royal Agricultural Show. Those top-hatted gentlemen of the Press tramped around the muddy showground by day and produced a daily twelve columns or so of comment and results. It is surprising they had much spare time left but in their hotel, the Old Black Swan in Coney Street, later in the evening the topic that recurred time and again was the difficulties they often encountered in carrying out their work: problems of access, of ill-found allegations of misreporting, of instances of distress involving colleagues and their dependents.

Two or three well-known Pressmen had died in straitened circumstances and the customary whip-round had been made for the benefit of their dependents. Could not journalists establish some sort of provident fund of their own to enable them to make provision against such contingencies, they asked.

Throughout their stay in York for two or three nights during the duration of the show the subject was thrashed out. There was nothing formal about their discussions: it was merely friendly gossip. But in their shop-talk there was unanimity about the need of an organisation 'for the purpose of mutual benefit and defence' and determination to bring it about.

There had been similar talk on other occasions when journalists had met together informally but at York in 1883 the discussion moved a stage further and it was decided to actually make an attempt to set up an organisation primarily to enable Pressmen to make provision against death or ill-fortune but also to safeguard and maintain their professional rights and privileges. Manchester was chosen as the most convenient centre for a beginning.

This was undoubtedly decided through the influence of Harry Flint, a reporter on the *Manchester Courier*, who lived at Pendleton on the outskirts of Manchester. He was an apparently unassuming man who had joined the *Courier* in 1876 and became its Chief Reporter in 1896, a post he held until 1905 when he left on the sale of the paper. The rest of his career was spent in freelance work for a number of technical publications but he remained an active member of the Institute in Manchester until his death at the beginning of 1928, serving on the district committee and for many years nationally on the council. He bore, it has been recorded, a distinct resemblance to the famous journalist and politician of that era, T. P. O'Connor, and was frequently mistaken for his more famous Fleet Street colleague.

It is surprising, as H. A. Taylor mentioned in his short history

of the Institute's first fifty years, published as a supplement to the
Journal in 1940, that nothing was said by Flint of the salaries,
hours and working conditions of the profession as topics in those
York discussions. In his history Taylor wrote:

> Dwelling on the peaks were men comparable in gifts and status
> to the most distinguished practitioners of the older professions.
> On the plains existed men whose intellectual endowments were
> not meagre but whose lot was summed up in the phrase 'half the
> wages of a compositor and twice the hours'. In no calling was
> there greater diversity of pay and in none aspiring to the status
> of a profession was there such a large proportion of ill-paid,
> overworked men.

Journalism then, perhaps more so than now, attracted men and
women of diverse qualities and aspirations. Editors were often
men of great influence in politics: those in Fleet Street were
courted by statesmen and politicians and wielded great power,
while in the provinces editors were frequently men of stature, both
financially and politically. Reporters too were able to influence
events: the exploits of foreign correspondents such as Henry De
Blowitz and William Howard Russell of *The Times*, who became a
Fellow of the Institute, and George Augustus Sala of the *Daily
Telegraph* were still fresh.

Provincial reporters, although more often than not ill-
rewarded, were nevertheless in an influential position: those were
the days of long verbatim reports when political reputations could
be made or lost not so much on what was actually said but on what
was reported, and this depended on the literary ability of the
reporter to report what the orators were supposed to have said.

J. A. Spender, who was Charter President of the Institute in its
jubilee year, was at this time embarking on his journalistic career
which was to develop in so distinguished a manner. At the end of
Trinity term in 1885 he went down from Oxford with no clear idea
of a career, but as his uncle by marriage had founded the *Western
Morning News* at Plymouth in 1860 and the *Eastern Morning News* at
Hull four years later, it was not unnatural that he should gravitate
to full-time journalism after a short period as private secretary to
his uncle. He became editor of the Hull paper before moving to
London and has described in fascinating detail life in a provincial
newspaper office in that era:

We went in at eight o'clock in the evening and for the next three hours were disposing of the local news and writing any leaders or comments that were necessary on local affairs.

Then the decks were cleared for the high politics. The London Letter came in a parcel by train about eleven and was supplemented by late paragraphs which were telegraphed. But our chief material was reports of public speeches, which poured in on a detestable 'flimsy' from about half-past ten till one in the morning. We were by no means in the first flight of provincial papers, but it never occurred to us as possible that speeches by Gladstone, Salisbury, Chamberlain or Hartington should receive less than the full honours of a verbatim report, and we were often in grave doubt whether we were doing right in reducing others to a column in the third person. Often we came out with five solid columns of the utterings of these eminent beings, and a terrible business it was to get them to press in coherent form. The 'flimsy' would be unintelligible or illegible; whole sheets would be missing and others wrongly numbered. In despair I have written and put into Mr Gladstone's mouth eloquent sentences which he ought to have spoken and which at any rate seemed necessary to make his peroration suit his exordium. And in the intervals of these struggles something called a leading article, attacking or defending the speaker, had to be written and sent to press before the last part of the speech had arrived.

Journalism was then truly a creative art, demanding a combination of literary ability, general knowledge and considerable powers of argument.

Advances in typography and typesetting – the new technology of that era – had made much easier the publication of long speeches and reports: hence the need for shorthand writers to match the speed of the typesetting process and fill the gaping columns as quickly as they could transcribe their spidery outlines. There was intense competition for appointments to the journalistic staffs of newspapers; as many as a hundred applicants would respond to an advertisement for a reporter at twenty-five shillings (£1.25p) a week.

The 'Americanization' of the British Press was in the future: the journalist at the time of the inception of the new organisation was a person who had to be capable of providing either verbatim or

descriptive reports, of condensing three or four columns of the
platitudes of politicans into a column – a task frequently
undertaken late at night in a bustling railway station or in a jolting
railway carriage.

They assisted others to organise by reporting their meetings
and offering suggestions for guidance in their columns but in their
own life and affairs they were unprotected and deficient of an
organisation.

So much for the background to the organisational stirrings of
Harry Flint and his friends. Their ideas were far from universally
adopted. Some of Flint's Manchester colleagues greeted news of
the plans coolly: they were, they said, Utopian. But Flint and his
friends persevered and by the turn of the year there was felt to be
sufficient support to justify the setting up of a provisional
committee to mould the plans into shape.

They met at the Blue Boar Hotel in Hodgson's Court, a quaint
old oak-beamed hostelry of which Dr Johnson would have
approved, where the then homeless Manchester Press Club was
temporarily accommodated.

Many years later, Harry Flint reminisced about those hectic
meetings of the pioneering provisional committee over which he
presided with shrewdness and benevolence.

The members of the committee were keenly intent on business,
but occasionally they tripped each other up on the smallest
matters and frequently warm discussions took place and
amendment after amendment was moved and discussed. On
one occasion the unhappy chairman had four or five deposited
on the table in front of him. It was of little use trying either to
soothe or coerce the movers. They were all in earnest – all out
for one object – influenced by the best possible motives. Who
could be angry with them? They were anxiously desirous to do
something for the benefit of their profession, and not to take any
false steps that might tend to damage the work they had in
hand. Hence the 'gag' was not introduced or even thought of,
and the guillotine would not have been tolerated for a moment.

The chairman just simply allowed the journalistic terriers to
worry each other until they were tired. Any attempt to suppress
them would certainly have been resented and the whole force
and effect of the zeal and the eloquence of the rivals would have
been turned upon the chairman. So he smiled and waited and

his patience was rewarded. 'Put the amendment, Mr Chairman', said the cool-headed Fergusson. 'Which of them?' I meekly queried in reply. 'Mine', 'mine', came from four or five parts of the room. The expected had happened. There was a warm argument then as to which of the amendments was first moved and it really appeared that two were moved simultaneously. The incident resulted in a compromise that was generally satisfactory and, amid hearty laughter, we went on with the proceedings.

There was much canvassing of support in the succeeding months until enough interest had been aroused to warrant the calling of a meeting to inaugurate a National Association of Journalists. The largest gathering of journalists ever held in the United Kingdom was drawn to the Queen's Hotel in Birmingham on 25 October 1884 and passed a resolution which read:

> That in the opinion of this conference it is most desirable that an Association of the journalists of the United Kingdom should be formed for the purpose of promoting and advancing the common interests of the profession, and this Conference hereby resolves upon the formation of such an Association, under the title of 'The National Association of Journalists', which shall consist of gentlemen engaged in journalistic work.

The resolution was carried unanimously.

Once agreement had been reached at that meeting on the setting up of an organisation, with a membership fee of half a guinea a year, there was considerable discussion about what might be achieved in giving aid to members in distress. The 'extreme desirability' of offering grants during unemployment and illness, help for widows and children, and loans to members compelled to move to distant locations for employment were mentioned in a resolution which set the founders the task of investigating these laudable objectives.

Harry Flint was elected the first President and within five months he and his committee reported that they had already assisted several members and sub-committees were looking at the establishment of a benevolent fund and the regular issue of a journal.

One of Flint's colleagues in these formative years was a

sub-editor on the *Liverpool Mercury*, Joseph Mason, who was also official reporter of the Convocation of York for twenty-five years. He took a prominent part in the inaugural meeting in Birmingham and was the 'father' of a Benefit Fund Scheme which operated for some years but was ultimately discarded in favour of the present Orphan Fund.

It is significant that a benefit scheme was from the outset considered the primary work of the new Association and as early in its history as March 1885 an eminent actuary, Mr Francis Neison, prepared a scheme providing for sickness benefit, annuities and life assurance with contributions on an actuarial basis. The scheme was discussed over a long period, but some of the members were timid of starting a benefit scheme with so comparatively limited a clientele. The later movement to secure a Royal Charter and the proposal to establish the Orphan Fund combined to push into the background a broader scheme of benefits, although the object was to a great extent realised by the introduction in 1898 of the Provident Fund and, in 1910, unemployment benefit.

Initially, the new organisation was primarily provincial. Although representation at the Birmingham meeting was national, London journalists had shown only passing interest, apparently being content with the provisions of the Newspaper Press Fund and the London Press Club, which had been started a couple of years earlier. But after some months and following a meeting at the Press Club, well-attended in the event, at which they heard a report from the President on the new association's aims and the progress that was being made, they began to take a decisive role in the affairs of the new organisation. It was at this gathering that mention was first made of a suggestion that the association would be a more acceptable organisation if it were to become an Institute of Journalists.

The response to the new organisation throughout the country was far from overwhelming. No doubt with the idea of attracting more London members and to exploit the interest shown at the London Press Club meeting, the first conference of the Association took place in Fleet Street in the former Anderton's Hotel in March 1886.

Outlining the early difficulties of apathy it was reported that: 'Strange to the idea of combination among themselves, although constantly urging it on others, working journalists were not easily reached or readily awakened to an active interest in the new movement.'

Three significant decisions were taken at that conference: the appointment of a salaried general secretary, with headquarters in London, was agreed; the establishment of a regular journal was approved; and Harry Flint, the modest, unassuming Mancunian who had worked so hard to get the organisation moving and had been its leader from the inception, handed over the presidency to a totally different breed of journalist, Sir Algernon Borthwick (later Lord Glenesk), the proprietor of the *Morning Post*.

The first two presidents of the new organisation were certainly extremes in the world of journalism. Borthwick was the eldest son of Peter Borthwick, editor of the *Morning Post* and had been virtually born into journalism. By the time he was twenty he had been sent to Paris as foreign correspondent of the *Post*. There, he had entrée to Louis Napoleon (later Napoleon III) and his circle. On his father's death in 1852 Borthwick had succeeded to the editorship, which he held for twenty years, and in 1876 had become owner of the paper.

Like many of his contemporaries he walked the corridors of power. He was a friend of Palmerston, who once declared that Borthwick was the only man fit to be Foreign Secretary. A year before taking office in the journalists' association he had been returned as Member of Parliament for South Kensington, which he continued to represent for the next decade until he was raised to the peerage as Lord Glenesk, the first newspaper proprietor to become a peer.

His position in Fleet Street obviously gave him influence but he never fulfilled the important role for which Palmerston had thought him suited. One of his parliamentary achievements was to secure an amendment to the law of libel which made it possible, where the same person brought two or more actions against different papers for the same libel, for the judge to order all the actions to be heard together.

The appointment of a general secretary in April 1886 marked a turning point in the organisation. The man appointed was Mr Herbert S. Cornish who occupied the office for the next forty years. Its immediate effect was a more rapid progress in membership, rules and economic matters such as fees for journalists taking official shorthand notes, and questions of Press accommodation in courts and facilities for reporters covering public events.

Another controversial decision was taken two years later. Four years had elapsed since the suggestion had first been made of the conversion of the National Association into an Institute of Journalists. Against some opposition to any change in the constitution it was decided at a conference in Bristol in 1888 to begin the conversion. These plans came to fruition a year later when, obviously primed of the imminent decision, the Lord Mayor of London invited the Executive Committee to hold its meeting in the Long Parlour of the Mansion House on 9 March 1889.

The committee then resolved:

1. That, in accordance with the instructions of the Special General Conference at Bristol on September 15, 1888, the National Association of Journalists be, and is hereby, converted into the Institute of Journalists and that the Bye-laws, as approved by the said Special Conference, be put into force and, from this day forward, supersede all previous rules.
2. That the draft Petition for a Charter of Incorporation, as amended by the Council, in accordance with the amendments of the Bye-laws by the Special General Conference, be and is hereby approved; and that the Committee of Administration be instructed to take the necessary steps for presentation of the Petition to H.M. the Queen in Council.

The momentous decision having been taken, there followed a spectacular reception in the Egyptian Hall to which the Lord Mayor had invited, besides journalists and their wives or husbands, famous men and women from the diverse worlds of art, literature and politics. Words, music and hospitality flowed in the manner which has become traditional in those elegant and glamorous surroundings.

Flint was a self-effacing man who was overwhelmed at the occasion and the distinguished dignatories from the literary and newspaper worlds who had been invited by the Lord Mayor. He stood at the rear of the elegant gilded hall undetected he thought by the distinguished platform party until, when the speeches were well advanced, the general secretary tapped him on the shoulder and delivered a message that the Lord Mayor wished him to go on the platform. He demurred but after a good deal of persuasion in which it was pointed out that, in those surroundings, a request from the Lord Mayor constituted a command, Flint hesitantly edged his way forward to the dais on which Sir Hugh Gilzean Reid beckoned him to share part of the large chair on which he was seated. When the speaker had finished, Flint was presented to the Lord Mayor who introduced him, amid loud applause, to the assembly. Flint was totally overcome when he was invited to speak. He later recalled:

I was totally unprepared and for a few seconds was speechless. There was more applause and Sir Hugh very kindly encouraged me to say just a few words. I screwed up my courage and with a desperate effort complied with the request. I expressed my gratification and that of my fellow pioneers at the success that had attended our labours. We had sown the seed. . . .

The occasion was a landmark in British journalistic history: it was also notable for another reason. In the drawingroom of the Mansion House Mr Edison's phonograph was reproducing the speeches of the eminent statesmen and others. The *City Press* reported:

Auditors were able to test the precise power of this new and curious instrument as the Lord Mayor made a little speech to Mr Edison which in two or three minutes was reproduced. The words were perfectly audible and all the stops and hesitancy were duly observed, but justice was hardly done to the Lord Mayor's excellent voice and there was something in the sound and intonation of the phonographic machine which irresistably reminded one of Punch and Judy. The voice seemed to issue from the recesses of a deep cave. Nevertheless, general surprise was expressed at the achievement of this wonderful instrument.

Harry Flint reflected on the memorable day as he travelled back to Manchester. It was an historic event. The hopes of the promoters were realised: the Institute of Journalists was an established fact.

The occasion marked the end of the first stage of the Institute's development and the beginning of a new era. Whatever the motives and ideals of the then leadership, that decision was to have a profound significance in later years: in receiving a Royal Charter it created an obstacle to successive future attempts to create in Britain one organisation of journalists. In effect, by preventing these merger attempts, of which more later, that original decision has ensured the continued existence of the Institute.

CONSOLIDATION

The Royal Charter of incorporation was presented to the council on 19 April 1890 and there followed a period of consolidation. The following February it was reported that membership was steadily growing throughout the United Kingdom: it was then 2500 compared with a mere 800 three years earlier.

There were some fears of a take-over by London members now that the headquarters were in the capital at 78 Fleet Street. There was, some thought, a danger of centralisation because of the difficulties of provincial members attending meetings in London of the Committee of Administration, the equivalent of the executive council.

London Region then had 700 members and it was felt it exercised more than its fair share of influence: it was even suggested that it was almost inevitable that London should exercise such a 'preponderating influence' as might imperil the permanence of the organisation. On the other hand it was argued that fears of a danger of the affairs of the Institute drifting into the hands of a few London members were unfounded. The London representatives could give close attention to the affairs of the Committee – and certainly many of them were men of some influence in public life – but, it was said, all these gentlemen were men having large sympathies with their provincial friends. Eventually, the President managed to assuage the fears and council meetings were subsequently held in different provincial cities.

The committee agendas give some indication of the wide variety of work the Institute was now undertaking. Apart from the routine domestic matters of administration and the setting up of a professional employment register, it was involved, among other things, in trying to remedy the exclusion of reporters from meetings of public bodies, including magistrates' and coroners' courts, uniformity in reporters' contracts, establishing custom over the termination of professional contracts, fees for journalists as professional witnesses and matters affecting libel suits.

Linage was another contentious issue, not only low payments for work undertaken but instances of the 'milking' by editors, sub-editors and chief reporters of copy written by colleagues and the exploitation of juniors by linage holders. A committee was appointed to look into the whole question. It was not only journalists who complained. A proprietor wrote plaintively:

> I employ an editor and seven reporters on a weekly paper. The editor (MJI) corresponds for daily morning and evening papers in neighbouring towns, the result being that 'exclusives' become almost an impossibility, every important item of news appearing in a daily before I can publish it. I keep the cow and my big neighbours milk it. I get the skimmed milk.

Another committee had earlier been appointed to look into the possibility of establishing a Benefit Fund and an orphanage. They sought more time to consider the Benefit Fund idea and were against an orphanage, but there was general agreement on the need for an Orphan Fund. It was established in 1891 with an original donation of £1000 from Sir Algernon Borthwick and one of £500 from Mr J. A. Willox, then editor of the *Liverpool Courier*, who was later knighted and became a member of Parliament as well as President of the Institute in 1895.

The fund, now the wealthiest of the Institute benevolent funds, still exists and in the intervening years has earned the patronage firstly of Queen Mary and, at present, of the Queen Mother.

The receipt of the Royal Charter undoubtedly put the Institute into the forefront of professional institutions. Contemporary reports of the meetings and activities of districts throw a fascinating light on the social habits of the period.

Meetings of districts were often held in civic surroundings at the invitation of the local mayor, and meetings were invariably followed by dinner and a 'smoking concert' and musical entertainment. Presidents of that period required a good constitution to do justice to the heavy round of dinners which formed such a prominent part of Institute activities. One example from Sir Algernon Borthwick's diary for February 1891 shows him speaking at the annual dinner of the Northampton district on a night when he also had an invitation to dine with Institute members in Cardiff and, in the same week, had invitations to dinners on the same night as far apart as Dundee and Belfast.

COMPETITION

Newspaper technology and news gathering techniques were changing rapidly. The Dover–Calais cable laid in 1851 had linked England and France in telegraphic communication. Three years later an Atlantic cable company was formed but the first attempts to sink a cable failed. Despite heavy financial loss, the company was not deterred and the *Great Eastern*, a former passenger ship built for Atlantic crossings, which had encountered various mishaps and bankrupted its owners, was saved from the scrapyard and adapted as a cable-laying ship.

Its saviour was Daniel Gooch, a former engine driver who had taken Queen Victoria on her first railway journey and had become a close associate of Isambard Kingdom Brunel, the engineer. Gooch's confidence led him to make an extraordinary offer to the cable company: if the ship failed to lay the cable there would be no charge but he would receive £50 000 of cable stock if she succeeded.

The famous war correspondent of *The Times*, William Howard Russell, was on board as the *Great Eastern* made its formidable attempt. 'as the *Great Eastern* moved ahead the machinery of the paying out apparatus began to work, drums rolled, wheels whirred, and out spun the black line of the cable and dropped in a graceful curve over the stern wheel', he wrote in one of his dramatic dispatches.

There were many adventures – faults involving cutting and rewinding the cable, technical snags galore – until the total loss of the cable and failure to retrieve it from the depths of the ocean brought the attempt to an unfortunate conclusion. Still not discouraged the cable company invested in a thicker and more complex cable and the next attempt, in July 1866 was successful – a great advance in international communications.

In Britain the development of the railways was complemented by the electric telegraph, the lines for which followed the railway system. Both improved communications: the railways afforded quicker delivery of the London papers to the provinces, while the electric telegraph resulted in speedier transmission of news.

A news service of sorts had been provided by the private telegraph companies but there was much criticism of its inadequacies and shortcomings, and demands for the nationalisation of the telegraph companies, which eventually came about in July 1868.

Three years earlier the Press Association had been formed, at a meeting in Manchester of newspaper proprietors, to organise a co-operative system of news collection and reporting. It was to be based in London, but the private telegraph companies proposed charging prohibitive rates for transmission. The provincial proprietors were quick to seize the opportunity presented by the new situation: further meetings were held in Manchester and London and the PA service was launched in November, four months after the state take-over of the telegraphs. Three months later they forged a deal with Julius Reuter whose agency, set up in London in 1851, supplied foreign news. The PA obtained exclusive rights to circulate his service in the provinces.

The other main news agency, the Exchange Telegraph Company, had come into operation in 1872 and wired financial and commercial intelligence to its subscribers. Its activities were extended in 1882 when it took over another company which provided a general news service. Political news was added four years later.

There were many other smaller news agencies springing up and individual journalists operating on space or freelance arrangements. With this number of rival agencies offering services to newspapers it was inevitable there should be bitter and ruthless competition. One area in which rivalry was particularly severe was in the Law Courts in the Strand. The Exchange Telegraph company was already accustomed to bitter competition on the race courses, another area of its operations, and on occasions these incidents were matched within the sombre surroundings of the Law Courts.

The incidents ranged between farce and high drama. An instance is recorded that during a civil action of great interest, a reporter from a rival agency installed a private telephone line in a lavatory so as to be able to contact his office with the result within seconds of the verdict being announced. But his efforts were thwarted by the Exchange Telegraph reporter who enlisted the help of a colleague whose task, successfully accomplished, was to lock himself in the lavatory at the crucial time.

The high drama came over Exchange Telegraph plans to develop its service from the Law Courts in 1891. It resulted in a complaint to the council from London district on behalf of one member of the Institute against another. The row developed into an important question of principle and, in a sense, a judgement on the new technology of the period.

The Institute was treading new ground. It was the first time such a complaint had been made: it was creating a precedent and there were no precedents to follow. Inevitably mistakes would be made and criticisms abound. The fact that the official report of the hearing occupied sixteen columns of close print indicates the seriousness with which the whole affair was treated.

The complainant, Mr William Collins, a member of the London District committee, was either a partner or an employee of a reporting agency in the Law Courts. He and other reporters there feared that any extension of the Extel Service would displace them. Indeed, they produced letters discontinuing the service they had provided to some evening newspapers in London. Collins complained that Mr J. F. Andrews, who was treasurer of the Institute and editor of the Exchange Telegraph Company, had been guilty of conduct discreditable to a journalist and tending to lower the status of the profession in violating the fundamental rule that journalists should not endeavour behind the backs of their brethren to obtain their work.

Mr Andrews had signed a circular letter announcing the improvements in the Extel Law Service to cater for the increasing demand for the rapid collection and delivery of news. They were proposing direct transmission from the Law Courts to subscribing newspapers by wire of up to five columns of reports of court-cases between 11 a.m. and 4 p.m., all within two minutes of the events happening.

The complaint had been lodged with the London district committee who urged the Committee of Administration to call a special meeting of the council to consider the complaint.

On receipt of a copy of the complaint Mr Andrews declared it to be 'so offensive that it is impossible for me to recognise the writer of it until he has apologised for the action he has taken'. The secretary, he suggested would no doubt deal with it 'as he would with any other notice which contained an unmistakable libel'.

And to the chairman of the Committee of Administration he wrote: 'If connection with the Institute exposes a member to the receipt of missives of this character membership will be something to avoid and not to covet.'

Extel, he explained, had been supplying law reports for some time and all but one of the six London evening papers depended to a large extent on its reports. The directors had decided to increase the staff and improve the service and had instructed him to write to the papers to ascertain how the proposals met with their approval.

'I object further that the field of journalism is to be closed against the march of progress and improvement', he added. That was a view also expressed by many of his supporters on the council. It was all a question of degree, they argued. No man had a right to go behind the back of another and try to cut him out of his employment by doing it for less money; but it would be absurd to say that an invention like the electric telegraph was not to be put into competition with the man who went on horseback.

On the other hand it was asked: was the Institute going to put its foot down upon that cut-throat competition which had already reduced journalism low enough and threatened to reduce it to a still lower ebb. This was no crusade against the introduction of new methods or mechanism, it was argued. It was simply an assertion of the principle that no member of the Institute should remain a member if he went behind the backs of other members to solicit their work.

One speaker graphically summed up the differences: 'The old service was carried on by a body of trained men who sent their copy by messenger to the newspaper offices; the new system was carried on by a flying squad, a few men who rushed from court to court picking up a piece of a case here and a piece there and rushed off to the wire with it.'

It was, in a nutshell, an example of the new journalism: the change from the unhurried preparation of long turgid columns of intelligence to the speedy acquisition and despatch of brighter news stories.

After four hours of deliberation, Mr Andrews was found not to have been guilty of any act or default discreditable to a journalist. The decision was decisive: twelve votes to three. The resolution adopted by the council added: 'This council is further of the opinion that it is not to the interest of the Institute to interfere in any way with the development of legitimate enterprise in journalism.'

That, however, was not the end of the affair. The London district complained that the council procedure had been incorrect in that the case had been decided without hearing the complainant, whereas Mr Andrews had submitted a written statement. They raised the findings at the following conference in August, when the council was asked to reconsider the complaint. The incident resulted in a procedure being laid down to deal with any future complaints of a similar kind.

The unfortunate incident released an icy blast of recrimination in which allegations were made of jealousy between provincial journalists and their London colleagues; of an elitism among the Law Courts reporters who systematically resisted attempts by journalists from the provinces to enter certain branches of reporting in London: one writer likened the law courts reporters to 'a family party who feel they ought not to be disturbed'.

It also brought into focus the growth and activities of news agencies. Since the abolition of the compulsory stamp on newspapers there had been an enormous improvement in some aspects of British journalism. The number of daily papers, as we have seen, increased: it was possible to obtain for a penny a newspaper which, for the quantity of material it contained and in the speed of publication of news, was superior to most of the newspapers which had cost 4*d* or 5*d* forty years earlier.

The cheapness of telegraphing coupled with the speed at which news could be conveyed had resulted in more information received by this method being used in newspapers: the cheapness of newsprint and the reduction in the price of newspapers had done the rest.

The transfer of the telegraph system to the state twenty years earlier had given a fillip to the publication of telegraphed news and the arrangement by which the Press Association had secured an advantageous tariff for transmission effected almost a revolution, particularly in the provincial press, which was enabled among other things to carry each morning extended reports of the previous evening's debates in Parliament.

These great advances in the quantity and speed of the material handled, however, brought disadvantages as well and there were criticisms that they were leading to a deterioration in the literary character of the newspaper, even in the area of leading articles, which were sometimes having to be written at 'break-neck speed' to keep up with events. This may have brought a terseness to the writing but was not favourable to elegance of style.

A slipshod style developed with the growth of the telegraphic transmission of news, it was claimed. Of the agency reports themselves, there were complaints of gross grammatical errors, that the agencies were transmitting trivia, that meetings were disposed of in an insufficient paragraph or two, and that the use of agency descriptive reports resulted in identical accounts of public events appearing in different newspapers, including some London papers which by then were beginning to use the PA service. 'In availing themselves so extensively of the agency system, the proprietors of newspapers, for the sake of a trifling saving, have done much to lower the standard of journalism', claimed a writer to the trade paper, *The Journalist and Newspaper Proprietor*.

There are still criticisms of news agency services, but few honest journalists would doubt that in the intervening years they have proved their value and worth and merit a respected place in the journalistic profession.

One of the criticisms of some news agencies in their early years was their use of non-journalists to supply reports. This was a practice also followed by some newspapers. In 1891 the Institute drew the attention of the Government to an instance in which a civil servant employed in the Post Office telegraph department was, during office hours, engaging in work as a newspaper reporter. To make matters worse he was also teaching shorthand at an institution at which the syllabus described him as a 'general, newspaper and Parliamentary reporter'. The practice ceased.

Members of Parliament were not averse to adding to their income from journalism and in the same year there was a call for a return to be kept of the number of MPs who 'eke out their income by writing for local and other journals what are called "Parliamentary letters" ', showing how many local papers published the same letter and the approximate amount of remuneration received 'for the gossip supplied or invented'.

Even ministers of religion were not immune. The *Shields Gazette* in 1896 regretted it was unable to report proceedings of the Wesleyan Synod meeting at North Shields since its reporter had twice presented himself for admission and been told the meetings were private. Yet this had not prevented reports appearing in the Newcastle daily papers 'not furnished through the ordinary channels of communication'. The paper explained:

> For some years now we have taken up an attitude of opposition to the practice, pursued by the Wesleyan Synod alone amongst legislative gatherings of Nonconformist churches, of refusing to admit professional reporters to their sittings whilst permitting ministerial members to report the proceedings for the Press for payment. Such a course is unjust to the public, since our experience has shown that reports so supplied are by no means always impartial, and is moreover grossly unfair to the representatives of the Press, many of whom are in this manner deprived of a portion of their livelihood. The Wesleyan Church is certainly not parsimonious in its treatment of its ministers and it is therefore all the more scandalous that some of those ministers should systematically do journalistic work in augmentation of their own stipends at the expense of hardworking professional journalists.

Through the determined efforts of the Institute certain sessions were subsequently opened.

Such practices eventually became rarer but it is more than a little ironic that the exclusion of Institute members from certain conferences, particularly those of some trades unions, should be an issue nearly a hundred years later.

In the 1890s these practices were so widespread as to lead the Institute into conducting an inquiry into the whole question of linage. They discovered that newspapers and news agencies were accepting copy from secretaries, members of public services, coroners, ministers of religion and other persons in positions of official authority and responsibility in preference to that of accredited journalists.

The committee formulated a code of practice which deemed it unprofessional for a journalist to use for linage purposes the copy of another journalist without compensation and urged newspapers and agencies to give preference to copy of accredited journalists.

By the mid-1890s the pressure of advertising, the low price of newsprint, and the invention of machines which added to the range of possible sizes all had a significant effect resulting in newspapers of larger size. The standard of education had been raised and readers' tastes were changing: the readership and demand for newspapers were, as a result, also increasing in unison.

The best reporter formerly was the one who could take the most accurate shorthand note to fill the acres of space devoted to verbatim reports of political speeches. Increasingly, as the century came to its conclusion, reporters were expected to be equal to any call or demand that might be made upon them – from covering a police court to a classical concert, from a fatal accident to an exhibition.

This was happening at a time when local self-government was increasing, when a growth in public speaking locally marked the transfer of some of the political turmoil from the national to the local scene.

Newspapers generally were becoming less uniform in their content and treatment of news. There was more individuality in these areas: newspapers were becoming brighter and more attractive and readable under the influence of the new journalistic innovators. The newer readers were less happy at being faced with a Sahara of close print in which the cross-headings of a sympathetic sub-editor were mirages rather than oases.

At Westminster it was the dawn of the era of the Parliamentary sketch writer: more readers were turning to this form of entertaining précis rather than reading several columns of a full report.

Interviewing of people in the public eye – and putting people there in the first place – was another contemporary development. The newspaper had become the mirror of the moving world and statesmen, men of letters, actors, artists and commercial magnates were all increasingly anxious to see their faces reflected in it. It was the new age of publicity and the newspaper was its instrument.

THE EXAMINATIONS DEBATE

In this changing journalistic scene the Institute's aim, as it had been from the start, was to uphold and maintain the standard of journalism and the journalist. The founders in setting up the Institute and its forerunner had cast envious glances in the direction of other professional organisations representing lawyers, accountants, chemists, doctors and civil engineers, and the granting of the Royal Charter had given impetus to such comparisons. The most significant difference in the case of journalists compared to the other professions, however, was the absence of any form of entry qualifications.

The founders' principal object was to raise the status of its members. If this was to be achieved, it was argued, some distinction must be created between members and non-members which might result in the latter being induced to join. A correspondent to *The Journalist* put forward a suggestion:

> The present policy of hunting up half-guinea subscribers on the highways and byways of journalism tends to reduce all members to the level of the least qualified person who can secure his election by a district committee. The way to raise our status is to close the door of the Institute to all who cannot plead adequate qualifications for membership. Let us treat outsiders as outsiders and discard sentimentality. It ought to be our aim to make the title 'journalist' apply only to members of the Institute. If that were done membership of the Institute will come in a few years to carry with it a *prima facie* claim for higher remuneration than that which is obtainable by the Toms, Dicks and Harrys who answer advertisements. I believe the Institute has the chance of doing for journalists as a corresponding organisation has done for accountants.

While that might have been a fairly extreme argument, there was nevertheless widespread support in principle for the introduction of an entrance examination but it was apparent from the start there were many difficulties to be overcome. In those other professions the examination was a technical one, while journalism was so complex, with so many branches and different kinds of work, that any scheme for a practical test was almost unworkable.

The task of formulating a scheme was handed to a special committee which reported to the 1892 conference in Edinburgh. While the main principles of the report were approved by a large majority in every division taken, it was ultimately referred back to the committee for re-submission to the districts with a view to reintroducing the whole question at the next annual conference. Thus began the period of foot-dragging which ultimately brought about abandonment of the whole idea.

The original proposal was for one examination of pupil-associates and another for admission to membership. In the former the candidate would choose from a list of six topics which did not require special or technical knowledge and write a paper of not less than 500 words on his chosen subject. The examiner would submit to the candidate twelve inaccurately constructed sentences to correct in a set time. The candidate would be examined in English history and literature, arithmetic up to and including vulgar and decimal fractions; easy question in algebra and the first book of Euclid; geography, especially of England and the British Empire; the translation into English of an easy passage of Latin, French or German, at the choice of the candidate; the condensation of a report from 1000 words to 200–300; the writing of paragraphs on three incidents briefly narrated by the examiner; and a summary of a balance sheet. Examiners could take into consideration a candidate's knowledge of shorthand but examination in this subject would be optional.

In the proposed examination for membership, candidates would be required to show proficiency in the English language; English Literature, constitutional and political history, political and physical geography; sufficient knowledge of Latin, French or German; and an acquaintance with general history. Mastery of composition and aptitude at condensation and précis writing were essential and every candidate would be examined in the principles of the law of newspaper libel and, in the case of general reporters, in verbatim reporting, condensation, descriptive writing and the conduct of the best-known branches of public and legal business.

The report had a mixed reception. After a year a revised scheme was submitted in 1893 which enabled a candidate to off-set proficiency in some subjects against shortcomings in others provided that overall he attained not less than a specified minimum number of marks. The scheme was approved and 1 January 1896 was set as the date on which the scheme should be implemented. There was, however, further argument, particularly over the need of a more technical type of examination, which led to a feeling that the time was not ripe for its introduction and the starting date was deferred for a further year.

Meanwhile the argument continued. By pressing the examinations scheme early in the life of the Institute they would be doing harm to the poorer individuals in their ranks. Conversely it was argued that the scheme should at once stop the stream of cheap labour exploited by inferior proprietors.

The number of more intelligent readers of newspapers had increased through the operation of the Education Acts and not only were there more readers but they were more critical and discriminating. Therefore, supporters of the scheme argued, those who served them should be careful to admit to their ranks only men who would be worthy members of the profession.

The debate revealed some interesting facets on journalistic recruitment. The staffs of many journals had come through the composing room. This was the case in several rural areas and, surprisingly, the staffs of a number of papers in Edinburgh had entered the profession by this route and, it was pointed out, had made splendid journalists.

So far as its literary content was concerned, the scheme was equivalent to the Oxford and Cambridge senior and junior local examinations, which was held to be of a comparatively low standard. Strong, though, were the demands for a more technical examination in newspaper practice but there were many difficulties foreseen in testing ability at sub-editing, leader writing and other journalistic tasks. Some saw dangers of a split in the profession, with a large body of journalists who had taken no examinations working alongside Institute members who had. Men and women would come into the profession without the examination and would be employed by newspaper proprietors whatever the Institute might think.

At the beginning of 1899 the special committee on examination tests was discharged. The brief motion was adopted without either comment or dissent. But that was not the end of the matter. A motion at the annual conference that year recommended to the council, pending operation of a compulsory scheme of professional examinations, a plan for voluntary examinations for pupil-associates or its sanctioning education tests for this category of entrant submitted by districts desirous of bringing about a higher standard of professional qualifications. The examinations committee, it was thought, had attempted too much: they had proposed a series of examinations for all classes of membership, found they had too heavy an order on hand and thrown it up.

Again the argument raged: should it be a voluntary or a compulsory examination. Some speakers thought the creation at that time of technical and secondary schools in the state system would render Institute examinations unnecessary.

Eventually, the secretary pointed out that the original scheme had been approved and was on the standing orders but the syllabus and administrative provision had been referred back and a date for putting the scheme into operations postponed. 'Next question' was moved and carried and the question of examinations went back into limbo.

The matter again cropped up at the conference the following year when Birmingham sought the adoption of a scheme devised by one of their members, Mr J. Cuming Walters, who went so far as to present a paper on the subject, in which he regretted that the subject had been allowed to lapse into a moribund state.

The subsequent debate resurrected the well-worn arguments and to solve the difficulties the President intervened with a motion stating that the subject of examinations should be no longer deferred, instructing the council to prepare a scheme, which for a short time would be voluntary, by making any necessary revisions of the previously adopted scheme. Some modifications were made by the council and it was decided the scheme should come into operation in a year's time.

For a long time it was thought that the exhortation in the charter to devise a method of testing the qualifications of candidates for membership was best met through a rigid examination system, but a new line of thought emerged at the Dublin conference of 1906 when the idea was floated that Trinity College would assist in the development of journalism by supplying special lectures for journalists or intending journalists.

The idea resulted in a shift of emphasis from examinations to the establishment of an *entente cordiale* with several other universities – Birmingham, Leeds and Glasgow among them – and Institute districts in the organisation of lectures, sometimes within the university curriculum. There was also discussion of a university preparation course in journalism and London University was induced to provide facilities for a degree course, which continued until the outbreak of the 1939 war.

The Institute's own examinations, despite the good intentions and the interminable discussions about them, were never a success. Abolition of the examination for pupil-associates was sought by Manchester in 1910: it was then argued that the test had only had the effect of driving young journalists into 'another organisation'. It fell to Harry Flint to move the conference motion. 'The journalist', he said, 'is born and not made', a view with which J. L. Garvin subsequently concurred. But the motion was defeated.

After the launch of the NUJ it was argued that for any examination to be of real use both organisations would have to make the passing of examinations a condition to junior membership. There was some support within the NUJ which itself contemplated some provision for ensuring that youths entering journalism had a good educational groundwork. One of its early presidents, Mr W. A. T. Beare, thought an entrance examination might be of great value to the profession.

> I think the Institute can eventually exercise an exceedingly useful function as an examining body. There would be nothing incongruous with such an Institute of Journalists as I have in mind in members of the Union being members of the Institute as well, for it would give them the hallmark of proved attainment and there should be no sort of conflict between the two bodies.

The subject continued to be raised from time to time but wartime was not the correct time to proceed with anything more than the voluntary scheme already approved.

The voluntary scheme turned out to be a failure. The general secretary, Herbert Cornish, said on a later occasion he had always been of the opinion that the decision to have examinations should have been taken years before and the difficulties grappled with and conquered.

It is interesting to speculate how the original intentions, if they had been implemented, might have affected the profession.

THE MEMBERSHIP DEBATE

In its early years there was no shortage of self-criticism within the Institute. Letters and discussion of its advantages and its shortcomings occupied many columns of *The Journalist and Newspaper Proprietor* and took up much time at district meetings, meetings of the council, and annual conference.

It was generally held that the Institute's existence alone had raised the tone of journalism and that the profession not only occupied a higher position in the estimation of its members but was better respected by the community at large as a result of the Institute's presence. 'The old spirit of Bohemianism and of Philistinism is extinct in the profession – that reckless and irresponsible indifference to duty which marked the profession twenty-five or thirty years ago has disappeared', said the president, Sir John Willox, as the century moved towards its close.

The inclusion of proprietors in the membership remained one of the most contentious criticisms: there was a feeling that control had passed to them rather than the ordinary members, an argument to which credence was attached by the succession of eminent proprietors who occupied the presidency in the years of its early growth.

Conversely, it was strongly argued that to have excluded proprietors would have been a disservice to the organisation. Harry Flint himself, the chief founder-member, apparently never regretted the decision. If they had been excluded, he said many years later, the organisation would either have foundered or have been set back half a century.

The question of the admission or non-admission of proprietors was fully discussed at the inaugural conference. Flint recalled:

All the arguments pro et con that could be thought of were brought forward and threshed out. There were proprietor-reporters and proprietor-editors and managers taking a lively interest in the scheme [for the formation of the Association]. The rank and file of journalists did not come forward in the numbers or with the enthusiasm anticipated. Many approved of the proposal and that was all. Not a few, while ready to obtain any and every benefit they could from the movement, left others to do the work and to divide the responsibility. Then again, the proprietors who were working with the committee were good, generous-minded men, and they were as much 'working journalists' as any of those who were salary-receivers. Why were they to be excluded?

Numerically, the proprietors were never strong. Out of some 3000 members around the turn of the century, 90 per cent were reporters and there were considerably fewer than a hundred proprietors. They certainly had no need of an organisation to protect their interests: the Newspaper Society had already existed for that purpose for some years. In the early days of the Institute, the minority – however small – undoubtedly exercised an influence in excess of their numbers but as they were invariably men already prominent in public life, many of them Members of Parliament, it was inevitable that they would take a leading part in its activities.

Whatever the rights and wrongs of the decision taken at the time, it is a legacy with which the Institute has had to live in the ensuing years. There is no justification for criticism nowadays when there exists an autonomous Salaries and Conditions Board to deal with salary levels and working conditions from which any member who exercises 'hiring' and 'firing' responsibilities is excluded. Nevertheless, the Institute has had to suffer even in recent times the ill-found allegation of being an organisation of proprietorial lackeys, a view not held, however, by managements nor the Newspaper Society and Newspaper Publishers' Association who have faced its negotiators.

Accusations of proprietorial taint reached a peak towards the end of last century. Journalists should, as far as possible, manage their own affairs, said Harry Flint at the July 1896 council meeting when, on behalf of Manchester district, he moved that council should hold it to be contrary to the original aim of the Institute that any office, whether in a district or sub-district or at the centre should be held by any but working journalists.

Strong complaint was made in the North of England, he said, that gentlemen other than working journalists had been elected to positions of importance in the Institute. Working journalists knew the requirements of the profession and it was felt that they were entitled to any little honour that attached to the leading positions.

Flint did not specify whom he had in mind. By the phrase 'working journalist' they did not mean exclusively men engaged in the daily and nightly round of journalism, he said, adding with propriety that they did not regard men such as Lord Glenesk, Mr Thomas Crosbie, Sir Hugh Gilzean-Reid and Mr John Willox (all recent presidents) as any other than working journalists. But it was to be regretted that men had been elected to high office simply on account of superior social position and their presence had acted as a check on the free and healthy action of the districts.

Flint did not succeed with his motion. It was rejected after strong argument that the phrase 'working journalist' was too vague.

The admission of newspaper proprietors continued to be a burning issue for several more years. In Manchester they were decidedly against it and sought the views of other districts in 1906 on a resolution on the advisability of retaining proprietors as members. In some districts, it was reported, their circular was 'treated as a dangerous explosive'. A ballot of Manchester members backed up their call, but there was a lack of support elsewhere. A Manchester district report stated:

> The result of the inquiries would show that whatever may be the views of journalists outside the Institute, the general body of journalists inside the amalgamation are not prepared at the present moment to welcome any movement for the exclusion of the proprietors.

TRADE UNIONISM

The main complaints at the time were that the Institute had failed to benefit working journalists, that its discussions were mainly of interest to editors and proprietors, that its social entertainments were too pretentious and its conference too expensive for ordinary country reporters, and that it had failed to improve the status of journalists and increase salaries.

Certainly it had spent too much time in discussing domestic matters and had extended the discussion on the proposed examination scheme over ten years with no result. Mr P. W. Clayden, President in 1894, believed too much time was taken up in matters of domestic organisation, such as the number of council meetings, powers of the executive, representation of districts and revision of the byelaws.

> 'We can only get and retain the attention of journalists, who deal with large affairs, by holding the wider aims of the Institute constantly in view', he warned. 'If year after year we are to be asked to give a week of precious holiday time to the consideration of such subjects, I for one would feel I would be far better occupied idling by the sea.'

There was pardonable impatience among many members at
the slow progress. What was being achieved seemed small in
comparison with the aspirations of members, who pointed out
that salaries had not gone up with a bound and conditions of work
were scarcely changed.

Some members counselled patience. Rome was not built in a
day, they said, and the Institute could not be built up in a decade.
Time was needed to allow the plant to grow: it should not be
perpetually pulled up by its roots.

The situation produced fertile ground for the argument that the
Institute should become a full-blown trade union. Impetus to
these demands for an aggressive trade union role was provided by
an incident involving industrial action which runs counter to the
general belief that Institute members have never been, nor would
ever go, on strike.

The strike involving Institute members took place at the offices
of the *Preston Herald* in April 1897 when reporters there left the
office because of the conditions under which they had to work.
Their action was backed by the Manchester district, which
appealed for help on behalf of the men concerned. 'Much
satisfaction was expressed at the prospect of intervention by the
Institute', says a contemporary report. 'It was felt that this was
essentially a case in which official recognition and help are
justified and it was hoped that the Institute might find in it
opportunity to initiate a policy of substantial aid under circumstances such as those which led to the strike.'

The incident was short-lived, every one of the reporters
securing better posts elsewhere but it was held up to be an
illustration of *espirit de corps* and an answer to critics who asked
what the Institute was doing for working journalists.

It did, at the same time, bring into focus the argument about
the Institute's role as a corporate body, an argument which had
preoccupied the founders long before the association came into
existence and one which persists still: is a journalist a professional
man or woman first and foremost or a trade unionist.

It was put in perspective at the time by Mr E. E. Peacock, one of
the London founders, when he said:

The organisers of the National Association of Journalists had in
their mind nothing more than a trade protection society for the
benefit of a limited class, associated with which it was proposed

to establish – as in the case of other trade unions – a provident fund. It was simply to have been a trade union for newspaper reporters of the United Kingdom but there were few of them who had gone through the mill of journalism for many years who had not become painfully aware of the fact that in their profession such an organisation was absolutely impossible, at all events under existing conditions. Journalism was so varied in its character and offered so much scope to originality and journalists came from so many classes of society that anything in the nature of ordinary trade unionism was impossible. The operations of the Institute of Journalists had to be far larger; they had to go beyond the lines of mere trade unionism and bring in all the elements which went to make English journalism a great profession – from the proprietor to the humblest reporter.

Had there been an earnest and overwhelming desire for a full trade union for journalists at the start, the founders had plenty of experience on which to draw. The printing trades unions already had a long history and had been in advance of their time in matters of organisation, a tribute to their better education than most other trade unionists of the era. They had imposed restrictive practices as early as 1587 and it was in the printing trade, almost a hundred years before the journalists got together as an organisation, that the first agreement on wage scales between proprietors and unions had been completed in 1785.

Manchester, where the idea of an association of journalists had been born and nurtured, had also seen the birth of the Trades Union Congress at a meeting of trades unions there in 1868. Initially the TUC had concerned itself mainly with legislation affecting the status of unions and the interests of their members. By 1874 its membership totalled one million in 150 unions but it suffered a period of stagnation in the 1880s because of industrial depression.

Having rejected all-out trade unionism as its basis and permitted membership for all engaged in journalism, the dilemma facing the originators and leaders of the new journalistic organisation was the nature of its role. The ideal was a truly professional organisation on the lines of other professions, but unlike them it lacked entrance qualifications and its long prevarication on the subject of examinations proved ultimately to be a lost opportunity which might have had a significant effect on the practice of journalism. As it was it took another fifty years before entry qualifications were introduced for the profession as a whole through the united efforts of the whole industry in setting up the National Council for the Training of Journalists in 1952.

An alternative would have been a role and position similar to that of the old craft guilds, combinations formed by merchants and craftsmen, employers and employed, for the promotion of common objects and protection of their members. It ended up as a hybrid of all three.

The inception and early years of growth of the Institute coincided with a revival in more militant form of trade unionism in 1889–90 in which there was greater agitation for a legal minimum wage and shorter working hours which itself coincided with the birth of socialism. These were factors which were undoubtedly reflected in the agitation in the Institute at the time over its performance and future role.

The charter had among its aims improving the status of journalists. While some progress towards this had been made from a professional point of view, members complained that there had been limited benefit in material terms. There was still widespread exploitation by unscrupulous employers using cheap labour.

An indication of annual salaries at the time is afforded by an extract from a magazine of 1897, which stated:

A reporter for a weekly paper seldom receives a higher weekly wage than is paid to a journeyman printer and frequently he is expected to assist either in the business department or the composing room. The salaries of junior reporters on the daily Press are not understated when they are set down as between £100 and £150. The more experienced men on the higher class provincial dailies receive from £150 to perhaps £250; while remuneration to the heads of the staff may range from £250 to £400, sometimes reaching £500 when special descriptive work, or art, or musical description is expected of them. The rate of pay of a sub-editor is on the whole a little higher; a few of the best men on the best papers get £400 or £500 per annum. Several of the provincial editors get as much as £1000 a year. This is the tip-top figure.

There were, the article added, many opportunities to journalists to augment their income by acting as correspondents of the London and county daily papers or through official note-taking in the courts.

Conditions were the cause of the Preston strike as we have seen. Other instances cited include a man who took up the post of reporter-editor of a small paper who discovered on arrival he was expected to 'fill in time at case', although nothing of this had been hinted in his interview or letter of appointment. As he knew nothing of composition in the printing sense, he was immediately dismissed. Such incidents were not isolated.

As the century closed the Institute's leaders had fudged the examinations issue and the question of improved salaries had been shunted into a siding, at least for the time being.

Both subjects were to recur and occupy many more hours of discussion in future years.

8   A New Century Begins

The early years of the new century brought some change in the
Institute's direction. Mr A. W. Still, editor of the *Birmingham Daily
Gazette*, who was President in 1903, directed much of his attention
towards salaries, particularly the introduction of a minimum
salary and the setting up of a Defence Fund. It was appropriate
that after launching his campaign on home ground in Birmingham he quickly followed it up with a visit to Manchester: the
district there had been desirous that a working journalist should
be elected president and Mr Still was of that stamp.

He saw the dilemma thus: when the Institute was founded it
might have proceeded on one of two lines. It might have set up a
high standard of examination and formed a select body so that
membership would become in time evidence of the holding of a
certain rank and dignity in the profession. That would have been
a practical policy. But the founders had hovered between that
well-defined policy and the opposite, but equally clearly defined
one, of bringing in all those who were in any way associated with
the practice of journalism. The Institute had vacillated between
the two.

Like his Manchester friends, Mr Still held strong views about
the position of proprietors as members of the Institute. No man,
he said, could be a member as a proprietor unless he was also a
working journalist and a proprietor who met that qualification
had as much right as any to membership. But the working
proprietor had no more right to special influence or a special vote
or any other sort of special power than the most ordinary and
humble member. As nine-tenths of the membership were simply
working journalists, the interests of the working journalist ought
to be constantly in their minds, aimed at in their policy and
secured by every force at their command.

The higher earnings of some printing workers compared with
many journalists is often mistakenly regarded as a fairly recent
phenomenon in the newspaper world, but attention was being

66

drawn to the existence of these differentials by Mr Still and others as long ago as the turn of the century and earlier.

The discussion provoked by Mr Still's pronouncements on the aims and policies of the Institute centred around the method of approach to the generally agreed aims: was it desirable to take up a trade union attitude towards the question of salaries and conditions of employment or approach them in other ways? His own suggested remedy was not trade unionism in the vulgar sense of lockouts, strike and big agitations for wage increases but the principle of mutual helpfulness.

Three or four years earlier William Newman Watts, then chief reporter of the *Blackburn Evening Express*, had begun preparing the ground for a national union devoted only to 'working journalists'. When he moved to the *Manchester Evening News* he found more encouragement, which resulted in a growing agitation for an organisation of journalists free of proprietors.

The agitation came mainly from journalists outside the Institute but some within it, particularly in the north-west area, felt it was hampered by its Royal Charter and joined in. It was a significant development in the profession versus trade union argument.

The advocates of trade unionism were now uncompromisingly blunt with those journalists who sincerely regarded their calling as a profession. Frank H. Rose, who contributed a trade union letter to Robert Blatchford's *Clarion*, wrote:

> If the average journalist will shed the silly notion that he is a superior sort of special creation and accept the bitter fact that he is just a working man, he will make it easier. There are hundreds of reporters and sub-editors who work longer hours for far less pay than the linotype operator or even the machine man in the cellar. He can put as much professional side on as he chooses, but he will keep going down industrially until he substitutes commonsense for vanity.

The open discussion on the Institute's aims coincides with, and was in part a defence against, the agitation on trade unionism. The advocates of a trade union circulated 'the working journalists of the United Kingdom' with proposals to set up a new organisation on trade union lines to be known as the National Union of Journalists open to 'all journalists (not newspaper proprietors, managers or directors) who are and have been for three years regularly engaged in the profession'.

Manchester representatives were at pains to explain that the Manchester district of the IOJ was in no way connected with the proposed new union of journalists and issued a circular of their own, which went to members nationally. 'Despite certain protestations of friendship on the part of its promoters', said the circular, 'the new movement is and must be directed against the very existence of the Institute. The two cannot exist side by side as effective organisations and it is for journalists to consider whether they will continue to give loyal support to the Institute, which has served them well at little cost, or help forward an organisation which may do less and will certainly cost a great deal more.'

What had the Institute done? Its Royal Charter conferred upon all its members the same legal status as other professional men and women and entitled them to the same fees when called upon to give evidence of professional matters in courts of law; it had set aside in its Defence Fund money for the express purpose of promoting the interests of members and defending them when attacked; it had established an Arbitration and Conciliation Committee to settle disputes; it had found through its employment registers employment for hundreds of members; its Orphan Fund had helped maintain countless children; its Provident Fund enabled members to purchase their homes on mortgage and provided the best insurance scheme in the country, as well as superannuation; it had provided benefits for out-of-work journalists; it had negotiated fees for shorthand writing and was constantly obtaining payment of members' accounts for professional services; and it had protected and provided a corporate voice in the maintenance of high standards of the profession.

The IOJ circular pointed out that the Manchester district had declared itself against the retention of proprietors in the Institute – one of the chief matters of contention between the two groups – and 'has of late noticed with satisfaction that proprietorial representation on the governing and executive bodies has largely decreased, while the tone of the Institute as manifested alike at conference, on the council and at district meetings, tends more and more to become an expression of the aspirations and opinions of working journalists'.

But these manifestations had come too late, particularly for those journalists who found themselves caught up in the euphoric atmosphere of the birth of socialism and the development of local trades and labour councils and the Trades Union Congress itself.

Ironically, the new union was, like the Institute before it, conceived in Manchester and born in Birmingham.

AN ERA OF REFORM

The influence of the Press in terms of thought and opinion was at its climax in the first three-quarters of the nineteenth century. By the early years of the new century there were many more newspapers but generally their influence was much reduced. The mental and moral development of newspapers had failed to keep pace with their mechanical development. There was now more appeal to the immediate and less thought of the abiding – a sacrifice of commonsense to crude sensationalism and of the honest truth to the telling headline.

In his presidential address to the 1908 conference, Mr (later Sir) Alfred F. Robbins, the first of a famous family of journalists to become President, set out his views on the preservation of journalistic standards. They are as applicable today as they were when he first delivered them nearly eighty years ago.

> If there is to be a sense of responsibility on the part of the individual journalist, it is essential that it should be shared in every department of the newspaper with which he is associated and that those for whom or with whom he works should do nothing to lessen his self-respect.
>
> No editor has a right to ask, no owner has a title to insist upon, a contributor doing that which, by lowering his moral tone, injures not only the individual but the institution of which he forms part. A 'good story' is dearly purchased at the expense of truth: no just cause is served at the cost of fairness: and it is impossible in the long term for the journal to retain influence or the journalists to stand well in the public regard if, for passing popularity or a snatching at success, truth and fairness are either ignored or placed so far in the background as almost to be lost to view.

It is a message that every editor, newspaper executive and journalist could usefully transcribe and keep always before him or her today.

The Press, by the turn of the century and afterwards, was also becoming far less political, not in content but in its ownership and support of particular politicians. It was more politically independent and, as a result, more commercial: newspapers were started as money-making ventures rather than, as formerly, political tools.

It was an era of Press reform: the so-called 'new journalism' led by W. T. Stead, T. P. O'Connor, Alfred Harmsworth (later Lord Northcliffe), C. A. Pearson and George Newnes – and the journalists who carried out their revolutionary methods – had caught on, albeit with a very mixed reception. The London based newspapers were becoming truly national newspapers, especially when they began printing duplicate editions in Manchester, a practice started by the *Daily Mail* in 1900 and quickly followed by others, and one which created competition with the larger provincial daily newspapers.

Methods of reporting were changing rapidly. The utterances of politicians while being reported more concisely than in the verbatim era were nevertheless more frequent and voluminous numerically, creating pressure on newspaper columns to a much greater extent than fifteen or twenty years earlier.

The interests of readers had also extended to other directions in addition to politics: the diffusion of wealth and education and the popularisation of literature, arts and science widened areas that had previously been the preserve of the few. Not only did newspapers have to broaden their horizons to incorporate these new areas of activity but journalists had also to adapt their skills to cater for the changes. There was more specialisation, more creative and colourful writing, more intelligent anticipation of events. The specialist writers like commercial and financial journalists, parliamentary lobby correspondents, the man-about-town gossip writers and originators of the public personality cult, were all expected not merely to report the latest information on what had happened in their respective areas but to become journalistic tipsters and forecast what was likely to happen as well as what was being talked about in the inner councils.

On some journals there was less inclination than formerly to insist that statements and comments had been carefully verified: a greater readiness to use copy merely because it was readable.

All these developments were taking place at a time when the spirit of commercialism in the British Press was growing stronger: when the extension of corporate ownership and the decline of political purpose increasingly magnified the importance of the counting-house and began to threaten the editor's sanctum.

Not unnaturally there was much concern that there were dangers in the new order: that truth might be sacrificed in the desire to be ingenious and enterprising or witty and entertaining.

These changes were demanding more of the journalist, in time as well as skills. This was particularly the case with regard to weekend working. There were more Saturday engagements to be covered and on Sundays sermons had to be reported: increasingly incursions were being made into the sacred Sabbath. This all left little opportunity for the journalist to have much social life of his or her own: indeed, journalists were almost social outcasts.

The increasing tendency of daily newspaper proprietors to work their staffs seven days a week was a matter of concern, but protests were even more emphatic when, in 1898, it was announced that certain newspapers – the *Daily Mail* and the *Daily Telegraph* in particular – intended to become seven-day journals. This was not a new phenomenon to the world of journalism: seven-day journals had been in vogue in the United States for many years. But their proposed introduction in Britain aroused much public discussion and a generally unfavourable reaction. It seemed they were not over popular in America either: the *Guardian's* American correspondent reported: 'The general opinion among intelligent people here is that Sunday papers are at the best a nuisance and at the worst a curse and contribute much to the intellectual and moral enfeeblement of thoughtless readers.'

After observing the public discussion and a more domestic one in London Region, the council pronounced emphatically against the idea. A healthy public opinion did the same and the idea was dropped. That year's President, Sir Wemyss Reid, editor of the *Yorkshire Post*, reported that 'those who were concerned in the project earned our gratitude by the alacrity with which they yielded to that opinion. The council took an active part in the agitation against the proposed establishment of seven-day journalism and I do not doubt that its pronouncement had its due weight with the proprietors who sought to introduce this undesirable innovation.' A resolution was carried by conference expressing 'its appreciation of the action taken by the proprietors of the *Daily Telegraph* and the *Daily Mail* in discontinuing the Sunday editions of those journals'.

While these years marked an era of reform for the newspaper industry and journalism, the first decade of the twentieth century was equally a period of transition for the Institute quite apart from the controversy over the methods of achieving its aims.

It was performing its rapidly increasing work in cramped offices above Barclays Bank in Fleet Street and many members had dreams of a palace of their own where meetings and social functions could be held, the administration of the Institute carried out and ordinary members meet in club-like surroundings. Negotiations started for a site in Tudor Street in the precincts of the old Bridewell Hospital.

Frederick J. Higginbottom, who was prominent in the acquisition of an headquarters building, has described how it was achieved. Higginbottom had made a name for himself as a reporter on the Press Association reporting from Ireland. He joined the staff of the *Pall Mall Gazette* in 1892 and later became editor.

For some years about the end of the century I took an active part in the administration of the Institute of Journalists of which I was an original member. I became one of its honorary secretaries, and took the initiative in the scheme for the erection of the present hall of the Institute in Tudor Street, Blackfriars.

The Institute was at that time housed in a few rooms in Fleet Street and I felt so strongly about this undignified arrangement that I determined to do what I could to change it. I proposed the appointment of a committee to consider a scheme for a building of our own and this was set up. It consisted of Sir Donald Straight, as chairman, Mr Samuel J. Fisher, Mr George Kynaston, Major Alex Steven of Berwick-on-Tweed and myself. A site was found in part of the ancient Bridewell at Blackfriars; an honorary architect, Mr E. Florence, designed the building, and it only remained to raise the money.

Some of my fellow committee-men were a little timid of the scheme, but I persisted and carried it through. About £2,000 was collected and the balance of £4,000 was obtained by mortgaging the building and creating a sinking fund for the repayment of the principal. The scheme was completed in 1902 and it has proved its practicability and its usefulness; while the sinking fund has worked automatically towards paying off the debt.

Mr Higginbottom, however, records only part of the story. It was a modest site and the proposed building fell short of the aspirations of some of the dreamers. It was scorned by some as being paltry and situated in a 'slum' area: others considered the financial implications to be hazardous: yet more objected to the spending of money on such projects until the Institute had succeeded in getting improvements in salaries.

Holders of these divergent opinions formed an odd alliance to fight the scheme: their suspicions were aroused by the inevitable secrecy with which such transactions are enacted and these were fanned by fears of a take-over of the organisation by newspaper proprietors who had subscribed to the building appeal.

The new headquarters, however, became a fact. The money problems were sorted out and the building remained the Institute's base for over seventy years until the balance of the lease was realised and the Institute offices moved in 1974 firstly to Whitehall Place and later to Bedford Chambers in Covent Garden.

When the headquarters battle was over, elements of the opposing forces remained on active service, particularly in the London region where a group known as The Reform Party took control of the committee in ensuing elections and vowed to make the Institute more useful to its members. Election campaigns between the opposing Reformers and the Progressives enlivened the proceedings in London for some time and served to revive the interest of some members who confessed they had not attended meetings for many years.

By the end of the first decade of the new century the Institute, which had then been in existence for twenty-five years, had outgrown its original basis and system of organisation because of the changing conditions of contemporary journalism and the consequent expansion of its work. A period of transition ensued in which the working parts of the organisations were subjected to searching inquiry.

There was at the same time much work on the protection of journalists' rights in relation to a new Copyright Act, a new Libel Bill and the effects of the complicated new National Insurance Act to contend with. A call for joint action on all these matters with the Union, with the supreme desire of promoting the interests of journalism, was made to the 1912 conference, an early attempt at co-operation with the newer organisation.

In several districts there was close co-operation with the Union on matters of general interest to the profession: in the north-east, which was to become a journalistic battleground some seventy years later, a special committee of the two organisations worked together whenever joint action could be taken. 'There is no reason why, because we differ somewhat in methods we should not pull together whenever we can do so for a common object', observed a columnist in *The Journal* of April 1913.

In the same year, the President invited representatives of the Union to join the Institute in a deputation to newspaper proprietors which reached an agreement on payments to sick journalists, probably the first occasion on which joint action was taken at national level. But while there was much to be said for co-operation in certain areas, there were many members who thought their colleagues who had reneged and supported the formation of the Union to have been disloyal to the Institute: they could, it was said, have better expended their energies on reforming the Institute and making whatever they would of it, thus avoiding what many thought to be the futility of having two organisations, both offering similar advantages to their members.

THE CHARACTER OF JOURNALISM

The dramatic growth of newspapers in the last three-quarters of the previous century had been checked by the early years of the new century. During the twenty years up to 1914 the total number of newspapers, morning, evening and weekly, in England had increased by only about 6 per cent, while in the same period the population had increased by 24 per cent.

There were then fewer morning and evening newspapers in the main centres of population than twenty years previously: the newspaper game had always been a competitive one but competition had been heightened by the innovations of the popularisers of papers. There were still many press barons around, but elsewhere there was increasingly not only more corporate ownership of newspapers but more multiple ownership.

These factors had a bearing on the competition: while the individual proprietor was a business man or woman who liked a profit, he/she did not have a responsibility to shareholders and usually preferred less profit to compromise with principle. On the other hand, under corporate ownership the concern of the shareholders, who were invariably investors and not journalists, was principally their dividends, with the danger that principle might be at peril.

Through the greater use of special newspaper trains and newer methods of distribution, the London newspapers had become truly national papers and the larger provincial dailies were having to face stiffer competition.

The advent of popular journalism was having an effect on the character of newspapers and on the people who wrote them. Increasingly the writing editor was becoming an extinct species: administration was becoming the dominant factor. Whereas a few years earlier there were great personal forces in journalism, with every leading newspaper having at the centre a writing editor from whom the lifeblood of the paper flowed, these forceful personalities were being displaced by an editorial organisation on the modern, widely circulated newspapers which was a superb piece of mechanism in which every department played its harmonious part.

The man of ideas in the news sense was ousting the man of opinions in the political sense. From the consumers' point of view, newspapers had become more readable, more attractive, and more entertaining. From the journalists' standpoint, there were better opportunities for a better remunerated place in the editorial hierarchy in return for which the work was more strenuous and stressful.

While a minority were highly paid, an inquiry conducted early in 1914 disclosed disgracefully low rates of pay among the majority of journalists, with most of those who sent in returns being paid less than £3 a week. On a great majority of papers there was no objection to reporters or sub-editors engaging in linage: this fact undoubtedly had the effect of keeping down the range of salaries.

Districts were consulted on what was to be done but apart from revealing that the principle of a minimum wage was thought to be unworkable little could be done at that time: more important events were on the horizon.

The threat of war had been looming and heavy responsibilities were placed on journalists in the exercise of restraint in what was published. Newspapers omitted many matters that came to their notice so as not to foment international difficulties. There were hints of the Government bringing in a Bill to curb the Press in times of danger, but it decided against such a serious encroachment on the freedom of the Press and wisely continued to trust the discretion of the journalists.

WARTIME

In May 1914 a number of German journalists were entertained to luncheon by the Institute Council. They were repaying an earlier visit by English journalists to Hamburg. Both visits were marked by friendship and hospitality.

One of the visting speakers at the luncheon, Herr Adolf Rey, said journalists had every reason to plead for friendship and good relations between the two nations and he sincerely hoped these good relations would continue and extend. When he returned to Germany he wrote of the visit: 'we shall do all in our power to foster and strengthen the friendship between Germany and England that these two brother nations may understand one another, and stand together for the maintenance of peace in the world'.

The expressions of good intent were too late. Three months later as Mr James Sykes, deputy editor of the *Yorkshire Post*, had a free weekend during which he settled down to write his presidential speech for the forthcoming conference at Bristol, crisis developed and he abandoned his presidential thoughts to return to his office. The crisis weekend was followed by an historic week of ultimatums and declarations of war.

The conference was postponed: it was eventually converted into a business meeting at the Institute headquarters. The Institute's affairs, like those of most organisations, came almost to a standstill apart from necessary work and a small committee was appointed to deal with emergencies arising from the war.

Censorship was imposed and for a considerable period after the declaration of war, Lord Kitchener and the War Office rebuffed pleas to allow war correspondents to proceed to the front line.

The Press Censors exercised their authority in a manner that was both capricious and inconsistent. It resulted in countless complaints and generally was held to be administered, at any rate in the early stages of the war, with the maximum inconvenience to journalists and the minimum of protection to the nation.

Early effects of the war on newspapers were mainly economic. The price of newsprint increased at an alarming rate for a time because of panic buying by a few companies, advertising revenues were drastically reduced, staffs volunteered for the Forces, a minority of employers reduced their staffs, and in some instances newspapers and magazines were suspended.

The accepted 'swings and roundabouts' of newspaper economics no longer applied in wartime conditions. Most newspapers suffered losses through the usual circumstances in which the volume of advertising suffered seriously while the cost of materials increased. An additional burden was the payment of allowances to members of staff who had gone off to war.

In the Crimean War the national conscience had been stimulated by *The Times* which had criticised the inadequacy of equipment for the severe conditions of that theatre of war. At the start of the 1914 war, Britain and France had been late in appreciating the values of heavy guns and shells, and Alfred Harmsworth, now ennobled as Lord Northcliffe, in 1915 emulated the earlier *Times* with an article in his *Daily Mail* in which he bitterly attacked Lord Kitchener over his choice of shells for the Army in France.

Editorial criticism of this kind was outside the censorship which was restricting the flow of news. The initial storm caused by Northcliffe's article subsided and public opinion came to his aid. Not even the Government held it against him: they recruited him as head of a mission which went to America and later he was put in charge of war propaganda.

TOWARDS A FUSION

Whatever the criticisms of slothfulness levelled against the Institute in its early days in delaying decisions on matters which members often thought demanded more urgent action, the launching of the NUJ had provided a stimulus to action and by the outbreak of the war there was general agreement that there was little to choose in the benefits each offered and that the aims of both were largely identical.

Feelings against the Institute appeared to be hereditary, based on conditions that had long ago passed away. The major difference between the two organisations was what was described by Harry Flint as the 'familiar old bogey' of the proprietors in the Institute membership. Was not C. P. Scott of the *Manchester Guardian* a working journalist? asked Flint. Was it not far better that proprietors and members of their staffs should meet on one common basis and discuss matters affecting the interests of journalism and journalists than hold meetings apart from each other and regard each other with distrust and suspicion? Proprietors had to be working journalists to qualify for membership, they were subject to the rules, and there had been no evidence of action detrimental to fellow members.

Even a past president of the Union, Mr F. E. Hamer, who addressed an open meeting on trade unionism in journalism sponsored by the Institute in 1916, agreed that the allegedly adverse influence of proprietors in the Institute had been shown to be a bogey – something which, when you got to close quarters with it was found to be far less terrible than was thought; whose terrors proved on examination to be largely imaginary; but something that frightened people and worked on their fears.

Another Institute member who had helped form the NUJ also pointed out that there were many members of the Union who were more influential in recommending employment or disposal of staff than many proprietors. Members of the NUJ might sincerely believe that the proprietorial element was totally absent from their ranks but he believed it to be more common than they were aware.

Many members from Presidents downwards cherished the ideal of one strong and representative organisation embracing all sections of working journalists. The similarities between the two organisations, the difficulties of wartime and the prospect of grave problems at the end of it were all good reasons for expounding the argument and from 1916 onwards the campaign in favour of a fusion gained momentum, despite a rebuff from the Union in refusing to join with the Institute in making arrangements for reinstating journalists at the end of the war.

MERGER ATTEMPT 1921

In the early years of the Union's development there were, within the membership of both organisations, many advocates of fusion between the two bodies.

'The sincere desire to bring about a united organisation is cordially recognised', the Union executive said in a statement in 1916. It added, however, a rider which was to become as much of a stumbling block to fusion, as it had been a matter of contention within the Institute since its foundation. 'So far none of the Institute advocates appears to admit the case for the elimination of proprietors, managers or manager-editors from membership. It must be said firmly and definitely that upon this point there can be no compromise so far as the Union is concerned.'

Some advocates were in favour of co-operation rather than complete fusion: already there were considerable numbers who were members of both organisations. However, the Union annual delegate meeting (ADM) in 1917, meeting appropriately in Manchester, scotched any ideas by accepting a resolution which stated emphatically that 'co-operation between the NUJ and the Institute of Journalists for any purpose is unnecessary and undesirable'. In 1920, however, the Registrar of Friendly Societies gave recognition to the Institute as a trade union.

In spite of the attitude of the 1917 union ADM there were many members of both bodies who retained the desire for an amalgamation. The Yorkshire district of the Institute held a strong contingent with this desire and as a result of private talks involving the NUJ President, Thomas Jay of Bristol and the Institute President, George Springfield, there came a proposal in 1921 that the two executives should meet. There was common agreement between them that there should be one organisation and qualifications for membership were drawn up and submitted to the two councils. These terms stated that members of the Institute who were proprietors, directors, managers or managing-editors may be associate members of the new organisation but would not be allowed to vote or speak at or attend meetings, except those of a social nature.

Five members from each side were appointed to draft a constitution and investigate finances, but the talks ended in deadlock. The Institute council regretted that a successful issue of the negotiations seemed to be impossible except on the basis of the entire obliteration of the Institute and the sacrifice of its distinctive principle of including in active membership all classes of *bona fide* journalists.

It appears to have been not only the question of membership that led to the breakdown in negotiations. A further stumbling block was the issue of affiliation with print unions and, more serious, with the Trades Union Congress. The NUJ had affiliated to the Printing and Kindred Trades Federation (PKTF), after a ballot on the subject, in July 1919. The question of affiliation to the TUC had been back and forth in conference motions for several years but a ballot in 1920 had decided in favour of affiliation. (Their membership was shortlived: two years later they withdrew over a proposal to subsidise the *Daily Herald* and stayed out until 1940.) A third decisive factor was the Royal Charter. A legal expert on trade union law Henry (later Lord Justice) Slessor gave an opinion that the charter of the Institute and the rules of the Union were incompatible and if the two organisations were merged the charter of the Institute would be liable to forfeiture. Dissolution of the Union would be unnecessary.

Before the final breakdown of this attempt, the council of the Institute put forward a counter-proposal suggesting the formation of a Federation of Journalists with the Institute and the Union as the founder members. The Union response was negative: it did not see what good purpose a federation would serve – it would mean a recession from the decision arrived at that one organisation of journalists was desirable.

1928

Experience had shown there to be fundamental differences between the two organisations that made impossible a straightforward amalgamation. Nevertheless one organisation of journalists remained a goal in the minds of many people in each organisation. In 1927, a second effort was made after the NUJ annual delegate meeting had declared its willingness to resume negotiations and the Institute council had welcomed the appointment of a joint committee to explore the possibility.

Three meetings were held at which a formula was worked out

which gave hope of a solution: a plan for 'the delimitation of the respective functions of the Institute and the NUJ'.

The formula was as follows: the Union whose membership would be confined to journalists who could not exercise powers of an employer, would provide machinery to deal with all matters relating to wages, hours and working conditions; the Institute would continue to operate as a chartered body for professional purposes. It afforded dual membership and put the question of affiliation to the PKTF and the TUC to a ballot of the enlarged NUJ.

The formula was accepted by the council of the Institute and the executive of the Union, and sub-committees worked out the detailed arrangements, but legal complexities then arose. Legal advisors of both the Union and the Institute considered there was nothing in the union rules to prevent operation of the scheme but all doubted whether the Institute could do so without surrendering the charter.

The view of an eminent independent counsel, Mr Stuart Bevan KC was sought. He summed up his opinion thus:

The Institute would be going outside its objects if it made membership of the Union a condition of membership of the Institute or if, in consideration of the Union extending its benefits to members of the Institute, it agreed to contribute to its funds, either by allocating to the Union part of the subscription of members or otherwise, or if it entered into any arrangement which was in effect an amalgamation or partial amalgamation with the Union.

9 Between the Wars

Economically, newspapers came out of the war in poor shape. The 'popular' papers were making money and could afford to pay their staffs generously but newspaper publishing generally was far from secure: it was losing money and in one period alone in 1920 over a dozen papers ceased publication within a few months. It was an ironic situation in which the number of newspapers was shrinking at a time when the market for them was expanding.

Individual ownership of newspapers in the past had strengthened the independence of the press: it had resulted in a preference for stability to stunts. But after the war individual ownership was becoming the exception and some of the old newspaper dynasties were disappearing, to be replaced by combinations.

In a material sense the advent of the 'popular' periodicals benefited the journalists concerned, but elsewhere the closure of newspapers and the grouping together of others led to fewer editorial jobs with greater competition and depression of salaries, which resulted in demands for a minimum wage.

One of the areas where there was much expansion was in the production of Sunday newspapers, a reflection of the decline of the Sabbath day.

The man who had been largely responsible for the rise of popular journalism, Alfred Harmsworth, died in 1922. In death as during his lifetime, the assessments of his achievements were controversial.

There appeared in the Institute *Journal* a strongly worded editorial article, written by George Springfield, the editor and a former President. Northcliffe, he wrote, was

Success personified; but what shall profit a man if he gain the whole world and lose his own soul – lose it in the sense of never manifesting or developing it? The lesson of his life is that material 'success' is not everything, however marvellous,

however brilliant. Lord Northcliffe's success in his own chosen
sphere was swift, absolute, complete, unprecedented. . . .
Before he was forty . . . he had become a millionaire proprietor
and a peer of the realm. He lived on for twenty years in the full
enjoyment of his success, and at the end was accorded the
solemn magnificence of a funeral service in Westminster
Abbey. He was a Napoleon without a Moscow. But with
opportunity unparalleled and with power uncontrolled, he yet
achieved nothing better than an influence with the unin-
structed or the unthinking of which he made no use but that of
the demagogue, to excite popular emotions and foster the
public's foibles, whims and weaknesses. Leadership with him
meant merely getting ahead of the crowd.

It was strong stuff, written at a time of customary eulogies. The
editorial caused an immediate storm of protest from prominent
members like William Latey, who had been a war correspondent
for the *Daily Chronicle* and was later to achieve distinction in the
judiciary. He was then chairman of the London district of the
Institute. Alan Pitt Robbins of *The Times* and Thomas Marlowe of
the *Daily Mail* both resigned in protest, although they recon-
sidered their decision.

In the changes in journalistic technique resulting from the
growing popularisation of newspapers, the influence of the daily
papers on public opinion, especially on political questions, had
diminished. The leading article had been devalued: whereas at
the beginning of the century and earlier up to four columns had
usually been devoted to leading articles, one column was thought
to be adequate twenty years later, and that expressed not, as
previously, the personality of the editor but the policy of the
paper, a collective view representing the combined wisdom of
several people, often including the proprietor.

Many of those closely involved in the changes were prominent
members of the Institute who have become legendary figures in
the history of journalism: men of the calibre of J. L. Garvin, editor
of the *Observer*, who was President in 1916, A. G. Gardiner, who
was editor of the *Daily News* and President in 1915, and R. D.
Blumenfeld, an American who spent most of his journalistic
career in Britain, editing the *Daily Express* for thirty years. He was
President in 1928.

Not unnaturally there were mixed views within the Institute

about the changes overtaking the profession. J. A. Spender summed up the scene in 1924 with these comments:

> If the older type of newspapers had suffered from the advance of the new type of popular newspaper with great circulations it was partly their own fault. They had carried immense respect and won for the British Press the unique reputation for seriousness and integrity which it enjoyed throughout the world but the absorption in politics and public affairs and the immense proportion of their space they had given to Parliament, public speeches and serious leading articles had narrowed their appeal to the public and cut them off from a great many human interests and activities which appealed to the rising generation and especially to women readers. When Alfred Harmsworth arrived on the scene offering a new type of paper with a brighter and more varied bill of fare, a million readers heaved a sigh of relief and went over from the old to the new. There seemed at first no reason why the new kind of newspaper should not exist alongside the old but this proved difficult. The more serious papers were bound to have a much smaller circulation than their popular and cheaper rivals and advertisers could not be persuaded that quality in circulation was equal to quantity.

The provincial press was more successful at that time in retaining its individuality. Arthur Mann, a distinguished editor of the *Yorkshire Post*, said that if journalists were false to their duty to the public – if they gave a biased and distorted view of events for political, personal or commercial motives, if they exaggerated the sordid, sensational and cynical side of human nature, thus giving a false view of the character of the people – then they risked the dignity and credit without which the journalist had no real influence.

Many of them did take that risk. One of the more serious criticisms at the time was the growing tendency not only to devote an undue amount of space to reports of divorce cases, murder cases and other criminal activities but to include in the reports the more salacious details of the case. It was a development which caused much concern within the Institute and offended public opinion to such an extent that a Bill was presented to Parliament to suppress the publication of these reports.

There was also a suggestion that journalists should have a corporate body to deal with any of their number who offended – what must have been one of the first hints at the future Press Council.

'Ghost' writing was another problem created by popular journalism. The publication of articles bearing the signatures of persons who had not written them was one of the features of the circulation battles of the popular papers in the 1920s: sport and theatrical personalities were among those usually selected. It was a practice deplored within the profession and one that was held to be indefensible and a fraud upon the public. The 'ghosts' usually received miserably inadequate payments for their work, while those who merely lent their names received substantial cheques.

The General Strike of 1926 put the trade union versus professional argument to the test. As soon as it was discovered that the entire services of the newspaper press were to be included in the strike, the Institute called on all professional journalists to exert themselves to the utmost to maintain the supply of public information through the newspapers and by all other possible means.

At the end of the strike it was reported that the council was not aware of any member who did otherwise than remain loyal to his professional undertakings. The same was true of the majority of journalists generally; a majority of members of the NUJ defied an instruction of their leaders not to help in bringing out emergency papers if 'blackleg' labour was used. Not only did journalists do their own work but also undertook that of others on strike like the operating of linotype machines, machine minding, packing and distributing papers.

The strike was held to have justified what many had been insisting for years – that a professional body could not be organised on a crudely trade union basis with all the conditions and implications that involved. It presented a crunch decision for many journalists: one of those won over by the institute's attitude was Mr R. V. Walling, who was a Union official in the Manchester district. Later in the year he was appointed general secretary in succession to Mr Herbert Cornish.

Competition for increased circulations intensified during the 1920s and 1930s and readers had to be bought. Doorstep canvassers were actively signing up new readers and outdoing each other with increasingly tempting bribes, usually offers of encyclopaedias and sets of books but also free insurance. It had happened before: back in 1891, for instance, the *Hertfordshire Standard* claimed to have found a happy method of sharing in charitable work (while at the same time boosting its circulation) by arranging with certain bakers in its circulation area to honour in the tangible form of a loaf of bread the presentation of a coupon cut from its columns.

But there had been nothing to match the offers and the circulation warfare of the inter-war period. The international crises of 1938 and the outbreak of war in 1939 ended the circulation battle. By then the interest in the news itself was sufficient to sell papers.

The competitive atmosphere of the 1920s was marked by the advent of another rival, the British Broadcasting Corporation. In the early days of broadcasting, only fragmentary summaries were given in radio news bulletins but its potential was seen by many as a serious threat to newspapers and the supercession of the broadsheet by the broadcast was predicted. The impermanence of the spoken word was an important factor in favour of newspapers and although the immediacy of news reporting by radio and later television have caused newspapers to reassess some of their approaches to news coverage, readers have remained loyal to the printed word.

From a journalistic point of view, radio and television have opened up a new area of the media and afforded increased opportunities to journalists, many of whom have transferred their allegiance from the printed to the spoken word. It has proved to be a lucrative recruitment area for the Institute, which now has a strong broadcasting division.

In the light of the subsequent development of radio and television, particularly the commercial channels, it is interesting to recall the comments of a certain Captain Richard Twelvetrees in a lecture to members of the Institute in Glasgow in November 1924. In visualising the future possibilities of broadcast news, he said, it had to be remembered that a newspaper was far more than a paper devoted to news. It was the most effective medium for advertising. He added:

> As no paper would stand much chance of success without the support of advertisers, it is difficult to see how broadcasting can be considered as anything more than a supplementary aid to

the newspaper, for if advertising matter were allowed to be transmitted by wireless in this country the future would be too appalling to contemplate. Even if different items were to be transmitted on special wavelengths, the difficulties of selection would still exist and in the midst of a soul-inspiring oration the sounds of a raucous voice proclaiming the merits of somebody or other's backache pills will not be considered a particularly welcome interruption.

The new medium was far from popular at first with newspapermen. The Institute council represented to the Government Committee on Broadcasting in 1926 that no further material extension of the system of transmitting news by broadcast should be sanctioned. No public demand had been expressed for a more complete broadcast news service, they said, and the public interest would undoubtedly suffer in direct proportion to the success of such a service in displacing newspapers.

As radio and later television developed there was increasing competition, which caused newspaper journalists to re-examine their techniques. The result was that by the 1950s there had been some effect on the character of the post-war Press. The most notable change was the development of the feature side of newspapers and some newspapers began to approximate more to daily news magazines than the traditional newspaper. There was also an extension of investigative journalism and the stories behind the news events. The appetite for actual news was sustained by the radio and television news bulletins, which had become more substantial and more frequent. What the newspaper reader was demanding was to know the background to the news of the day as well as the news itself.

Although unemployment was rife among journalists, circulations of newspapers were reaching record levels: in the early 1930s the aggregate circulation of the national daily and provincial papers, together with Sunday papers, was estimated at 29 million. The diminution of newspapers had also been halted, although competition was intense. More money than ever before was being diverted from the improvement of production and salaries and conditions for the journalists into expensive circulation stunts which saw the degrading distribution of free washing machines, pyjamas, pillow cases, silk stockings, fountainpens and watches to those who could be induced into taking out a subscription. It was estimated there were 50 000 canvassers on the streets of Britain urging people to buy the papers they represented: many of them played on the sympathy and emotions of potential readers by pleading tales of poverty unless they secured a sufficient number of new readers.

Journalists were not the only ones to suffer through the depression: another casualty was Oak Hill, a large house at Ipswich, which had been given to the Institute in 1927 for use as a convalescent home for journalists. The donor was Mr T. R. Parkington, a local alderman and old school friend of the Institute general secretary, Herbert Cornish. After five years the home had to be closed because of the high cost of its operation and a falling off of contributions towards its upkeep. The residue of the finances after its closure were placed in a benevolent fund to maintain convalescent journalists which still perpetuates the name of the abandoned home.

An attempt was made in the mid-1930s to introduce a state register for journalists, such as existed in some other professions. The term 'journalist' would, under the scheme, have been reserved by law to those whose names were on an approved register controlled by a representative body set up by statute.

The idea had been proposed in 1931 as a piece of presidential kite flying, to which there had been a negative response and the financial crisis in the country that year precluded an approach to the Government. The matter was resurrected in 1933 when a deputation saw the Home Secretary. Criticism that it was an attempt to close the profession were firmly denied and the use of the word 'state' was perhaps a mistake since it raised the spectre of Government control, something that was abhorrent – indeed it still is – to most journalists.

The terms of the proposal would have applied to all journalists, but the NUJ voted against it, although H. A. Taylor, one of the forces behind the idea, claimed that its discussions had proceeded on little information and consequent misconceptions about the plan.

Proponents of the plan proceeded despite this rebuff. The Journalists (Registration) Bill received the approval of the council and in 1935 parliamentary efforts were made to get it enacted.

The Bill made it an offence for any unregistered person to use the title 'journalist' and contained a disciplinary clause providing for the striking off the register of any journalist held, after a disciplinary inquiry, to have been guilty of disgraceful conduct in their capacity as journalists. The register would be administered by a Journalists Registration Council consisting of members appointed by the governing bodies of the Institute, the NUJ, proprietors' organisations, unattached but duly registered journalists, and the senates of universities awarding diplomas in journalistic studies.

The Bill was regarded as an instrument for making journalism a true profession and in 1936 it was presented in the Commons by Sir Percy Hurd, but it failed on that occasion to proceed further. There appeared to be a real chance of its enactment in 1937 when Mr (later Sir) Alfred Bossom, who had reintroduced it, was successful in the ballot for Private Members' Motions and agreed to introduce the Bill. He was, however, unsuccessful in obtaining a hearing and, as a period of crisis ensued followed by the outbreak of war, further action on the proposal receded, although it long remained an ambition of many within the Institute and would have provided a safeguard for journalism in general and *bona fide* journalists in particular against the intrusion of unqualified people claiming, with dubious motives, to be journalists.

Among the journalistic developments at this time were the increased space being devoted to sport and the greater interest in foreign news shown by the popular newspapers.

In his presidential address in 1932, Sir Emsley Carr presented a vision of the future of newspapers: looking back one cannot but marvel at the remarkable accuracy of his prophesies:

I see larger and brighter papers and I see the introduction not only of coloured supplements but the advancement of illustration by means of photogravure, colour and additional line and artistic work. The art of publishing will be improved by the extensive use of the aeroplane. Wireless and television will be a commonplace both for news and pictures, and speeding up in mechanical production will be followed by a further development of worldwide news. The additional expense to meet these great reforms will be met by the ever increasing demands by the advertisers upon our space.

Another factor which has to be taken into account is the competition of broadcasting. I do not think that broadcasting will materially affect the position of the newspaper Press. . . . The spoken word will never replace the printed word.

10 Wartime and Beyond: the Merger Debate

Members and officials of the Institute were assembling in Belfast for the annual conference on the eve of the declaration of war. The conference was cancelled and replaced by an annual meeting in London a month later.

As the prospect of another war had approached, contingency plans had been discussed by the Government and to some extent implemented. The mistake of setting up a Press Bureau like that of 1914 was not to be repeated: it was thought wiser to keep censorship as part of a wartime Ministry of Information with a Cabinet minister at its head.

A committee had been set up to establish a register of journalists for service in the Ministry of Information but when was war declared and the Ministry began operations it took considerable badgering of Government departments before action was taken on the list that had been prepared.

The need for journalists to be used in the Ministry's press and censorship departments, whose work was described as 'the fourth arm of modern warfare', was stressed at the annual general meeting soon after the outbreak of war. The meeting was held in the board room of *The Times*: reports of it record that 'the meeting reached the hour of the blackout and the proceedings were therefore closed'.

Representations, which eventually proved effective, were made to Government departments for fuller and freer access to the sources of official information and the wider employment of journalists within the ministry and elsewhere in publicising the war effort.

Despite the war, the fiftieth anniversary of the incorporation of the Institute was celebrated in March 1940: a telegram was received from Buckingham Palace conveying congratulations from the King, the council was entertained to luncheon by the Lord Mayor of London at the Mansion House before their meeting, a wreath was laid at the foot of the memorial erected by the Institute in St Paul's Cathedral in 1905 to thirteen journalists killed in the South African War, and the Archbishop of Canterbury preached a sermon at a commemoration service in St. Bride's Church.

Just as journalistic techniques had changed, the techniques of warfare had also advanced and communications had improved. More fighting fronts demanded more war correspondents: the dangers were greater and war correspondents had to undergo special training before leaving for the front.

With the wartime Parliament acting largely as a mechanical machine of approval of the acts of the Coalition Government, there was greater urgency for the Press to maintain its right of criticism, albeit within the disciplines of war. Mr Clement Attlee, then Lord Privy Seal, defined the Government's policy as one of interfering as little as possible with the liberties of the Press to express freely their opinions and comments on the conduct of the war or on supposed peace overtures. But, he said, it must be recognised that statements could be put out in the guise of comment which either gave information of value to the enemy or were calculated to impede the war effort by weakening the resolve of the public and no assurance could be given that the publication of such statements would not be interfered with.

Fleet Street was a prime target for enemy bombing and many offices suffered damage but production of newspapers continued under difficult conditions, as it did in other parts of the country which were under attack. Tape machines continued to tick throughout all the commotion and staffs adapted themselves remarkably to the emergency conditions.

In one particularly fierce attack on the City of London on 29 December 1940, the journalists' parish church of St. Bride's was reduced to ruins by fire bombs. Many Institute members played important parts in the post-war restoration of the church, notably a former President, H. A. Taylor, who was chairman of the restoration committee.

Although traditional news sources throughout Europe suddenly dried up on the outbreak of war, they were replaced by the proximity in geographical terms of the effects of the war. With smaller newspapers, the preparation of reports and headlines demanded new guidelines: brevity in the wordage was the key and extravagant displays had to be curtailed.

MERGER ATTEMPT: 1943

The 1943 merger attempt came about through the initiative of the president of the Newspaper Society and the encouragement of the Printing and Kindred Trades Federation.

The initial move came from Mr W. T. Bailey, acting informally and without even the knowledge of his Newspaper Society colleagues, when he asked Mr Clement Bundock, the general secretary of the NUJ, whether it would be possible to meet unofficially with members of the Institute to see whether some way could be found to end the state of affairs. Bundock explained that the Institute charter remained the chief stumbling block. The NUJ was decidedly cool to the suggestion and subsequently the executive decided that in view of the earlier efforts at mergers they could not undertake the initiative in re-opening negotiations.

Mr Bailey did not lightly give up his idea. He discussed it informally with officials of the PKTF who then informed the NUJ they considered that nothing but good could come from entering into any talks that might be arranged. This changed the attitude of the NUJ executives who agreed to meet informally with members of the Institute.

Lord Rothermere, Chairman of the Newspapers Proprietors' Association (NPA), then stepped into the drama: he was host at a luncheon for representatives of the two organisations, which was also attended by Mr Bailey and officials of the PKTF, from which emerged a desire on both sides to produce, if possible, one united body to represent the interests of journalists.

Reports were made to both executives and, with their agreement, talks got under way. They were held under the chairmanship of Mr George Isaacs, a Labour Member of Parliament and chairman of the PKTF. While no criticism was made of Mr Isaacs's capabilities as a chairman, there was a feeling in some quarters that his trade union and political affiliations did not give him total impartiality.

The question of unity between the Institute and NUJ at this time was given impetus by the decision of the NPA to give recognition to the Institute as a negotiating body.

By the following February (1944) the bulletin of the PKTF was referring to trade union attitudes of those who advocated some form of fusion between the two organisations.

The trouble between them, it said, was not one of the 'kiss and be friends' type: it was a difference of principle. It rightly stated that:

> Through the whole history of the two organisations this difference in principle has existed. The present situation is only an exacerbation largely caused by the employers' organisations recognition of the Institute for negotiating purposes.
>
> How is the difference of principle to be overcome, for it must be remembered that the dispute has widened and that this Federation too shares in the difference of principle. Whilst the NUJ is capable of speaking for itself as to their requirements before 'harmony in some form or another' could be reached, it is impossible to believe that such 'harmony' would be at the expense of the trade union principles or would involve their agreeing to something by which they could not be affiliated to this Federation.
>
> The unions of this Federation could undertake no recognition of an organisation which continued to hold the charter which the Institute does. This dispute, while still primarily between the Union and the Institute is certainly one in which the unions in this Federation as a whole are now concerned.

Meanwhile at an official level talks were taking place between the two organisations to see whether practical steps could be taken to secure unity in the profession.

After a secret session at its annual conference the NUJ delegates approved a statement 'giving general approval to the steps taken to date by the union's representatives on the joint negotiating body and empowers the NEC to proceed with the necessary steps to submit a scheme, which may be approved by the joint body, to the judgement and decision of the whole union'.

Special meetings were called for 30 June that year (1944) to consider proposals for a merger. But an indication of the opposition that was likely to ensue from sections of the Institute council came in a letter, published in *World's Press News* on 17 May from Mr A. T. Penman, a distinguished member of the Institute in which he disclosed to all that there had been 'not inconsiderable opposition' to the proposals at the council meeting at which the President, Mr Harold Ffoulkes, leader of the Institute delegation, had moved that the proposals be approved. Before the council's discussion was completed, however, that motion had been amended to the innocuous and simpler proposition that the suggested scheme of fusion should be submitted to a general meeting of the Institute on 30 June without an affirmation for or against.

When the proposals had first come before the Institute council, those who disliked the scheme had been prepared to give authority for negotiations to continue provided other schemes were not excluded and other possibilities examined. What irked the opponents was the fact that when the Institute delegates reported on the further negotiations nothing was brought back to them but the original scheme worked out in greater detail.

The opposition to this proposal was lively and effective. It manifested itself around four members of the council: Eric N. Davis, H. J. Gregory Pearce, A. T. Penman and H. A. Taylor.

Archie Taylor had been President of the Institute in 1938, a product of provincial journalism before joining the old *Daily Chronicle*, where his career was interrupted by the 1914–18 war. In 1923 he had become chairman of Newspapers Features Ltd, a position he held for almost forty years. At the time of the merger talks he was MP for Doncaster.

Penman had had a distinguished career with Reuters, which he had joined on leaving school. Within fifteen months he had been sent to represent them in South Africa where he became vice-president of the first Journalists Association of South Africa. Subsequently he left Reuters to join the London staff of Argus South African Newspapers.

The four opposing councillors contended that, while there was scope for two organisations, each with its distinctive characteristics, acting in co-ordination to serve the profession, unity could not be achieved by the highly controversial methods which were being put forward.

Their main objections were that the proposals involved dissolution of the Institute and surrender of its charter, with the consequent risk of forfeiture of £100 000 in funds to the Crown, that there was no guarantee against NUJ members dominating the new organisation, and nothing in the proposals to eliminate the possibility of the new organisation affiliating to the TUC.

The four set out their objections fully in a letter to all members in which they said:

It is important that members should realise that these proposals involve nothing less than the dissolution of the Institute and the surrender of the Royal Charter, with the attendant risk of forfeiture to the Crown of the entire assets of the Institute, a matter of about £100,000 accumulated by the efforts and sacrifices of members during a period of sixty years.

In return for these surrenders, the membership of the Institute is to have the privilege of joining a new trade union, of which the present membership of the NUJ will have control, by reason of substantially greater numbers. Once this new body ('this enlarged NUJ' as it was described by one councillor) is formed the conditions of the merger will have no force. They do not constitute an enforceable agreement. The Institute having ceased to exist, could not resist any proposed breach of the understanding on which the merger had taken place.

One of the conditions is that the new trade union may enter into affiliations provided they are not with a political body. Whether the Trades Union Congress, to which the NUJ has been affiliated for many years, is a political party is not worth argument. We all know what it is and to what political party its powerful influence has always been lent.

The president of the Institute as a member of the negotiating committee on fusion (whose chairman was a trade union official and Labour MP) has admitted that there is nothing in the terms of fusion that can prevent the affiliation of the new body to the TUC.

Further, we are obliged to assume that NUJ membership would act as it has done in the past, and secure the affiliation of the new society to the TUC. Assumptions to the contrary are merely wishful thinking, unjustified by the evidence of the past.

Unity within the profession is a worthy ideal but the crucial point for consideration now is whether it is desirable to create unity in order that the sole organisation of journalists in this country shall be an ally of a particular political party. In that connection it is relevant to recall that at the last assembly of the TUC, the secretary, Sir Walter Citrine, spoke of 'This mythical thing called the freedom of the Press, this abstraction . . .' and added: 'We shall watch with great care in the next few days how these newspapers behave towards this Congress and we must carefully consider the situation in the light of what happens during the coming week.'

There are other aspects of the proposals for fusion which are open to serious objection. Moreover, the two legal opinions on them, which the Institute has obtained, leave considerable doubt whether the Institute can be dissolved for the purpose in view and whether, if dissolution can be achieved, the assets of the Institute can escape forfeiture to the Crown.

In our view it is fantastic to suggest that unity on matters of common professional interest can be secured only by methods so highly controversial and by running risks so grave. But there is scope for the two organisations, each with its distinctive characteristics, acting in co-ordination to serve the profession.

It is possible that the project will strangle itself in its own legal complexities but that process would take appreciable time, during which the interests of the Institute would suffer gravely from uncertainty about the future.

The letter was a reasoned argument against the proposals and had the desired effect of opening up discussion among members. One district, Manchester, unanimously decided that the terms presented in the draft report could not be accepted. In the light of subsequent events they were to prove prophetic.

When the proposals were discussed at separate delegate meetings on 7 July 1945, they were unanimously approved by the NUJ who agreed to submit them to a ballot of members with a strong recommendation that they be accepted. At the Institute meeting delegates merely resolved to submit the proposals to a ballot vote.

In international politics, the Potsdam conference was occupying the headlines. In domestic matters, journalists were pondering on a dilemma: would the proposed merger ensure a moderate policy within the new organisation by adding the Institute members to the moderate-minded NUJ members and thus together overcome the growing extremism of the NUJ? Would the moderates in both organisations outweigh the extremists in the NUJ who put politics before the welfare of the profession and those in the Institute who feared any change in its Royal Charter.

Opposition within the Institute gained force when the four council member signatories to the circular letter set up, at a meeting the following month in the Hall of the Institute in Tudor Street, an Institute Defence Movement. H. A. Taylor was elected chairman. The aim was to secure rejection of the proposed merger scheme because it amounted to the death warrant of the Institute.

In the following months, the Institute defenders prepared for battle. They were not prepared to rely merely on the legal complications surrounding the surrendering of the charter, formidable though they appeared, to scupper the proposals. They decreed that, in the event of the Privy Council being approached with a view to the surrender of the Royal Charter, they would declare their willingness to accept responsibility for maintaining the existence of the Institute in accordance with the terms of the charter and the byelaws and to administer the funds according to the various trust deeds.

'Such a declaration would probably result in the Privy Council deciding that the IOJ should continue', said Mr Taylor. 'There might then be a temporary weakening of the Institute but in perhaps not many years the other body might well be so reckless that there would be a reaction and the IOJ would get a big influx of members.'

The merger discussions at this time coincided with a change in the law permitting civil service unions to affiliate with the TUC. The defenders had no doubt that the proposed new association of journalists would also affiliate. It was consistent with the traditions of the civil service to affiliate with the TUC – 'a body ancillary to the new (Labour) Government' – there would be no diffidence about journalists doing the same, but no one who believed in freedom of the Press, it was argued, could put the journalistic profession and the only journalistic organisation in the pocket of the Government.

The ingrained apathy of journalists generally when it came to ballots was seen as a threat to the proposals. A 50 per cent vote of the membership of both organisations was stipulated by the Trade Union Amalgamation Act of 1917, with a 20 per cent majority of those in favour for the proposals to succeed. It must have been with some relief to the officers of both organisations that the necessary percentages were met when the result of the ballot was declared in January 1946. In the NUJ ballot, 5301 voted in favour and 165 against, a majority of 5136 for the merger: in the Institute voting was much closer – 695 for the merger and 559 against, a majority of 136 in favour.

The negotiators then got down to detailed discussions on the implementation of the proposed merger. The legal complexities which Archie Taylor had suggested might strangle the new-born child soon after its birth quickly became apparent and it was clear that patience would be a virtue. 'Fusion may come but it is a long way off', the Institute general secretary, Stewart Nicholson, commented the following July.

By then the Institute had sought a new legal opinion. The original intention had been to draft a supplemental charter authorising the Institute to carry out the proposed merger, but the new legal opinion thought this was not advisable before a draft scheme had been prepared by the joint committee drawing up the constitution and rules for submission to an inaugural conference. Counsel proposed procedure by means of a private Act of Parliament – a method which would obviously take considerable time.

However, the council of the Institute set up a small sub-committee, consisting of the then president Mr (later Sir) Linton Andrews, Mr Alan Pitt Robbins, the treasurer, and Mr Nichol-son, to examine the possibility of the private Act with the NUJ.

The legal opinion, extending to 5000 words, was prepared by Mr J. B. Lindon KC and Mr Colin M. Pearson. In it they said that dissolution of the Institute and transfer of its property to some other body would seriously affect the position of members in relation to its property and its various funds. Dissenting members might reasonably object to the grant of a supplemental charter at that stage when there were no specific proposals for safeguarding or providing for their interest in the property or giving them equivalent rights or expectations of benefits as members of the proposed new association.

The matter was complicated, they said, by special problems regarding the status, operation and destination of particular funds in the event of a dissolution of the Institute which presented considerable difficulty in connection with the general proposals.

In view of the numerous problems and difficulties they advised that the most convenient course would be to promote a private parliamentary Bill to incorporate the new association, to dissolve the Institute and the Union and to provide for the adoption of the provisions governing the various funds. Incorporation of the new association would balance the loss of the charter.

This opinion created a new situation. What was now proposed was not a variation of the draft proposals but an extremely important addition introducing new elements for safeguarding assets and continuing the funds.

'A way which has been difficult has perhaps become more

difficult as a result of the smallness of the majority in favour of the draft proposals but it must be followed and the duty of implementing the majority decision must be fulfilled', said the President.

The new sub-committee, it was pointed out, was appointed to discuss with the NUJ the one new factor of a possible parliamentary Bill. Meanwhile the negotiators from both sides were thrashing out the problems of fusion and drafting the constitution and rules of the proposed new association.

In the few months between the result of the ballot and October 1946 they held ten lengthy meetings in which, according to a joint statement issued by the general secretaries, substantial progress had been made and agreement reached on many important points. The meetings, it was said, had been notable for the eagerness to co-operate in the interests of journalists. They were facing a mass of detail but no effort was being spared to reach agreement and to produce a satisfactory constitution with the least possible delay.

The negotiators divided themselves into various sub-committees reviewing different aspects of the merger, finance, organisation, membership and rules. It was a complicated and heavy task demanding much attention to detail. It was also confidential: there were pleas for patience from both the Institute President, Linton Andrews, and the NUJ general secretary, C. J. Bundock.

There were official protestations of goodwill and good spirit in the joint committee but outside there were allegations of intimidation and coercion to prevent journalists becoming members of the Institute even while the discussions were in progress. Instances were quoted of open hostility towards the Institute: it reached a head at the annual meeting in October in a motion from London district calling for strong representations to be made – there were in the debate demands for the breaking off of the negotiations. The motion was withdrawn only after assurances from the president that representations would be made by the Institute negotiators.

It was at this same meeting that a new president was elected, none other than A. T. Penman. He declared his intention to maintain the strictest impartiality over the merger and with that in view announced his resignation from the Institute Defence Movement. He hoped members would approach the matter with less heat, less conservatism and a greater desire to reach a particular goal than they had done in the past.

The following April, the joint negotiating committee suggested another change in the method of achieving the merger. They recommended, after discussions with the solicitors representing the two unions, that a joint special delegate conference should be convened to adopt the constitution and rules, and that the conference should appoint the existing negotiating committee to sit simultaneously to deal with any disagreements arising at the conference.

Their reasoning was that the proposal to proceed with the merger by means of a private parliamentary Bill was a departure from the procedure accepted in the ballot, which had provided for the rules and constitution to be submitted to an inaugural conference and any disagreements arising to be referred to the first executive meeting of the new association. The legal advisors considered that the two organisations should adhere as closely as possible to the procedure accepted in the ballot.

No inaugural conference could be held as the new association could not be incorporated until the proposed bill was passed.

By July of that year, the negotiating committee was getting within sight of a draft constitution but there followed a three month deadlock in the negotiations. The issue was over safeguards against attempts at political affiliations on the part of the new association.

Officially it was said the negotiations had reached a 'delicate' stage. Behind the scenes the argument centred around political affiliation. The draft proposals agreed in May 1945 on which the ballot had taken place barred affiliations with a political party. The latest difficulty was a proposal put forward by the Union which, in the view of the Institute negotiators, might have the effect of weakening the safeguard adopted in the ballot. The Institute was unyielding, deadlock ensued for three months, until the NUJ, in the interests of speeding up the negotiations, modified its demands.

On the Union side the deadlock was attributed to the Institute's insistence on safeguards rather than an attempt by the NUJ to introduce a politics clause. 'We agreed to certain words going in solely for the purpose of removing the fears of the Institute about politics', said NUJ president Ernest Jay. 'My council was able to authorise that because, as has been repeatedly said in reply to this kind of statement, we are not and never have been a political organisation.'

The deadlock had been removed by the Union's acceptance of an additional object in the parliamentary Bill permitting variations of the other twelve objects by a 75 per cent majority at a general meeting provided, among other things, they did not include any political objects. Thus assured, the Institute council gave the negotiators authority to continue the talks without delay.

The joint committee completed the main part of its work and the preparation of the parliamentary Bill was in the hands of the lawyers. 'Notwithstanding difficulties that have had to be overcome, the Committee have carried out their work in an atmosphere of friendly co-operation,' said a joint statement from the two general secretaries. 'Patience and goodwill have resolved one question after another and harmony has been achieved in a body of rules that provides a good working basis for an association which would unite the organised journalists of the country.'

The final hurdle was not yet passed. Announcement of the completion of the talks coincided with the only meeting that year of the Institute Defence Committee. Mr Taylor said the plan rested on 'a split hair' – namely, the agreement that although the proposed new terms prohibited affiliation to any political party, the new organisation would be free to affiliate to the TUC as that was not a political party. But it was, he said, the parent and paymaster of the Labour Party, which had been born of a resolution passed by the Congress at Plymouth in 1899. The TUC were part owners of the *Daily Herald* and supported the Labour Party financially. A second objection by Mr Taylor's committee was of allegations of left-wing political influences in the ranks of the NUJ.

On this question, a columnist in *Newspaper World*, the trade magazine, commented:

One has to admit that there has been evidence of left-wing tendencies (I put it no higher than that) among the more vocal and active attendants at certain union branch meetings. This, of course, can be quite fairly turned against those who argue that such a condition of affairs demands rejection of the merger. A combination of moderate influences might well be the answer to any suggestion of left-wing domination. It is no good running away from the danger. But, merger or no merger, there is already evidence that many journalists who hitherto left union work to the enthusiastic few are at last realising the need for counteracting activities. . . .

Both organisations balloted their members on the parliamentary Bill. Although the result showed both to be in favour, the Institute vote was below the requisite 75 per cent majority in favour.

Immediately informal talks took place between the parties to see if the situation could be retrieved but six weeks later the Union executive unanimously decided there were no grounds for a resumption of negotiations and to speed their efforts to secure 100 per cent NUJ membership throughout the country and recognition of the Union as the sole negotiating body.

Many within the Institute felt too much time, money and effort had been expended on attempting a merger and that it should now concentrate on its own affairs and exert its influence in bringing about reforms that would assist journalists.

1966–71

Relations between the two organisations were at a low ebb: the NUJ even banned co-operation in organising joint social functions for charities. Yet within both organisations there remained members whose goal was the creation of one organisation for all journalists. Those within the union suffered a rebuff in 1952 when a conference motion seeking a re-opening of negotiations was rejected, although delegates did not endorse another motion calling on the union to abandon the object of a merger.

During his presidency of the Institute in 1956, Mr Alexander Boath frequently advocated the need for one professional organisation. A letter appeared in the NUJ official newspaper in July 1963 from Mr Kenneth Dodd, then of Manchester, advocating a merger and reconstitution of the Institute as the professional body responsible for education, training, ethics and professional conduct. It appeared beneath an article by Trevor Evans, the *Daily Express* industrial correspondent, on similar reforms then taking place in other trades unions and employers' organisations.

The following month two print unions, the Typographical Association and the London Typographical Society amalgamated. William Rees-Mogg, then treasurer of the Institute, took the opportunity of these developments to raise again in an article on the main leader page of *The Sunday Times*, of which he was then Deputy Editor, the question of journalistic amalgamation. He noted that in recent months there had been a notable and encouraging diminution in the word warfare that had characterised the relationship of the two bodies. Without defining too closely what degree of association ought eventually to be achieved, it was clear, he wrote, that it would be for the benefit of journalism if the two bodies could agree to co-operate.

> In any case it seems obvious to an increasing number of journalists that the two bodies would be stronger working together than they can be apart, and that it is disgraceful that they should quarrel with each other. . . . There must be an organisational structure more suitable for journalism than the present bickering division between two admirable, hardworking and otherwise responsible bodies. An associated or united body would give working journalists the power to protect their own professional standards; it would also help to represent their interests in an industry which is now on the verge of automation.

The Rees-Mogg article brought a union response through Tom Bartholomew, then treasurer of the NUJ. 'Theoretically, it is easy to make a case for one organisation', he said. 'In practice, it is far from easy to determine what kind of organisation can be created which will attract the necessary amount of support from the members of both organisations. A lot of time and thought has been devoted in the past without success in trying to thrash out a mutually acceptable formula.'

The first moves towards the next merger attempt were made at that year's Institute conference at Southport when Keith Gascoigne of Birmingham proposed a resolution urging the council to investigate the possibility of setting up a joint standing committee with the NUJ to consider matters of common interest. It was adopted with a London amendment adding the words 'and in particular the possibility of reaching an agreement similar to that drafted in 1928 providing essentially for the continued existence of both bodies but with a substantial dual membership and defined spheres of activity'.

The Institute was not yet prepared to go further. Another

motion in favour of taking soundings on the question of all journalists being represented by one professional body was heavily defeated.

By early 1966 proposals had been agreed for dual membership in an interim period while a parliamentary Bill was prepared for the disbandment of both organisations and their reform into a new association with a constitution incorporating the basic characteristics of both. A private parliamentary Bill was necessary because of the legal complexities associated with the Institute's charitable funds. Under the arrangement the Institute ceased its trade union activities and dealt with professional matter for the two organisations.

A *Sunday Times* leader bearing the hallmark of William Rees-Mogg thought this latest merger attempt had a better chance of success than any of its predecessors.

The proposals for joint membership and a division of responsibilities were approved by ballot and special meetings of the two bodies, and came into force at the beginning of 1967. Meanwhile, the negotiators got to work on the details of a proposed merger through the creation of a new National Association of Journalists, with an autonomous National Professional Council to control all professional as distinct from union activities, and which would be responsible only to professional conferences in which employing members could take part.

Inevitably the status of the proposed Professional Council led to difficulties. Although both teams of negotiators were agreed it should be autonomous, the NUJ executive refused to accept this and made counter-proposals, which were rejected by the Institute, that it should be elected by the NEC of the new organisation and act as an advisory council to the NEC on professional matters. This difference within the NUJ led to the resignation from their negotiating team of three former NUJ presidents, Kenneth Holmes, Allen Hutt and Denys Tuckett.

The status of the proposed council was an important matter of principle and was one of the three main points of fundamental difference which scuttled any hopes of a merger in the final act at Southend at the end of October 1971 of a five-year drama.

George Glenton, who was President at the time and had the unenviable task of being joint chairman on that ill-fated occasion, writes of that dramatic period in the Institute's history:

At 5 p.m. that day – October 30th, 1971, those IOJ members who had for so long become increasingly and, in many instances, fervently divided on the issues involved, were reunited. They stood shoulder to shoulder, brought staunchly together again by the political intransigence and intolerance of that section of the NUJ which clearly wished only to swallow us up.

The 'Trial Marriage' which some IOJ members had welcomed and which some had suspected or opposed, but which many members of both organisations had enjoyed through their dual membership, was ruthlessly dissolved in the moments it took to vote on a single emergency motion.

The stresses and strains of those seven years had, inevitably, increased as the proposed rules for a 'National Association of Journalists' were debated and compiled for submission to that Joint Delegate Conference. Debates within the IOJ in the months preceding that confrontation – the penultimate step before the proposed ballot of members – had become increasingly divisive.

Strong beliefs, genuinely held, made stern protagonists of old friends. The eagerness of some for an ultimate formal wedding to create a new single organisation under its own rules was matched by the obvious foreboding or forthright opposition of others.

There were those with long and loyal service to the Institute who were sincerely committed to the ideal, and those who had given it equal thought, but who baulked at the very idea of inevitably surrendering the Institute's unique Royal Charter.

Even where traditional bonds of principle might have once guaranteed agreement, fear and hope clashed over the possible interpretations of some of the proposed rules and over the absence of others. The Closed Shop was only one of such sensitive issues.

Ever since my election as President-Elect, at the Jersey Conference, in 1970, the atmosphere of contention had grown with the clash of honest argument and sincerely held opinions.

The Institute's Hall in Tudor Street was certainly no place to go for a quiet discussion at that time. Meetings took on a new excitement. They were frequently quite heated as points were strongly pressed and just as strongly challenged, but no doubt those splendid oak panels had echoed to much of it before if not so extensively.

The tension increased when it was announced in the first weeks of 1971 that the Privy Council had granted a Supplemental Charter on the application of the Institute empowering it to promote the parliamentary Bill needed for the proposed merger with the NUJ.

Council meetings had frequently been lively occasions, long before the merger talks had opened, but as the conclusion of the negotiations drew near almost every item of business offered some opportunity for contending factions to promote their views.

The great challenge was not to be taken by surprise by some of the more remarkable motions and amendments. To be even-handed required concentration and detachment which was not always easy. Another unusual feature was that original NUJ members were entitled under the rules of dual membership to be elected to the IOJ Council.

Several of them were diligent attenders and forthright participants. The same rule entitled original IOJ members to be elected to the NEC – the NUJ's comparable body – but it was an unlikely possibility.

On the whole I am sure our NUJ members enjoyed being there. I am sure they must have found it as invigorating and perhaps as educational as did their IOJ colleagues.

During those long last months of negotiations the number of meetings and the amount of paperwork was extraordinary. Every dot and comma had to be studied, and often debated. The time put in by the General Secretaries and staffs of both bodies, and by the officers of both organisations was phenomenal.

There were other calls beyond the normal duties of the Presidents of both. We had to attend each other's Conferences for one thing. In May I had to address the assembled delegates of the NUJ at their ADM in Bournemouth. Among them I was happy to see many journalistic friends with whom I had worked, and with whom I had sometimes argued over the years. They gave me a generous hearing when I outlined the doubts in the minds of some IOJ members over the safeguards they would expect in the draft rules to be proposed.

It was an opportunity as I saw it to warn those on the other side that the decision to merge or not, would ultimately still be in the hands of the individual members of each organisation and was no foregone conclusion. Sooner than I expected I was to face many of them again under less happy, less tolerant circumstances.

My deep concern in those months was shared by many others who recognised increasingly, as I did, that if the merger idea failed, the temporarily reduced role of the IOJ would leave it extremely vulnerable.

It was a problem occupying the minds of some of those members who most favoured a merger. For those closest to it it was a nagging worry, but the emotive issues of the moment left little opportunity for discussing contingency plans as widely as otherwise. To duck on such impossibility would have seemed to some – defeatism. That was the reality of it.

As I was to discover later, members with diametrically opposed views on the merger were, none the less, of a single mind when it came to restoring the Institute's viability as a professional body, and its credibility in its resumed trade union role.

The battle over the merger terms and the draft rules did not stop for a moment during Conference Sessions in Malta. In-fighting seemed if anything, even more intense.

But it was the survival of the Institute that was uppermost in many minds that week in spite of the memorable distractions. Looming large on the programme when we got home was the Joint Delegate Conference arranged to be held over two days in Essex.

The preparations for it had occupied much time and thought in those weeks when the arrangements for the Malta Conference were being finalised. When the final agenda for the Joint Merger Conference was presented it contained approximately 25,000 words.

Its 38 pages covered 28 proposed rules for the 'National Association of Journalists'. Among the long columns of amendments from NUJ branches and IOJ districts were twelve seeking to change even that neutral title.

Much of it had been debated hotly already by the Institute's Council and between IOJ Council Members and those of the National Executive Council of the NUJ at an all day meeting in a London hotel the previous November. The voting on that occasion had been based on a special standing order laying down that no resolution would be effective unless the majority vote in both Councils – counted separately – was in favour.

A similar rule was even more essential at the Southend Conference because of the greater numerical disparity in representatives. Under the different practices involved, the Institute fielded a team of less than 40. The NUJ delegates totalled more than 200.

It had never been doubted by the NUJ negotiators or those from the IOJ that such a system would be approved. It became almost the first bone of contention and quickly indicated the style and intensity of the debate on which the outcome of that important conference depended. A voluble body of NUJ delegates sought to deny even that concession.

From the platform where the Chair alternated between the President of the NUJ and myself as President of the Institute, it was plain to see from the opening shots that the proposed merger was an issue as passionately dividing the ranks of the NUJ as those of the Institute, but much less tolerantly.

The fact that at the end of the day every individual member of each organisation would be entitled to vote on whatever proposals emerged, before any new organisation of journalists could come into being, seemed entirely forgotten. Immediately one could sense dismay in those NUJ members who staunchly supported IOJ insistence on fair play.

Just as plainly I could feel the closing up of the Institute's ranks as intolerance in certain quarters threatened the goodwill now so clearly on the defensive. At one stage, reluctantly, but with the unspoken backing of every IOJ representative I was sure, I threatened to lead our delegation from the meeting if the proposed rule on voting was rejected.

At another stage of that stormy meeting I had to take over the chair to referee a motion from NUJ delegates that their own President, loyally uncompromising Douglas Rees, should stand down in favour of another nominee for joint chairman. It was rejected by 131 votes to 121, a narrow enough margin in that atmosphere.

If the Institute had needed reassurance in its approach to jointly founding a new association of journalists with old antagonisms buried, there was none that day. By lunchtime the stark reality was overwhelming. The Conference on which so much hinged had the carpet pulled from under it. Extreme militancy from a section of the NUJ had taken care of that.

The chances of the rules being approved in time to be lodged with Parliament by November 27, which was the aim, were virtually nil. It could have ended there, but there were slight hopes that a lunch break might bring a cooling down. It did not. By that time too many scales had been removed from too many eyes.

The afternoon proceedings were as contentious and have been well reported. There was a clear consensus of opinion to bring that dramatic confrontation to a halt. The NUJ delegates had voted heavily to retain the title of National Union of Journalists for the proposed new body. The IOJ members had voted for it to be named the National Association of Journalists.

The IOJ had lost out on the proposal to register the new organisation under the Industrial Relations Act – a most important issue. Next the opposing delegates overwhelmingly voted to delete the proposals for a National Professional Council to deal with matters other than remuneration and conditions of employment. They also threw out any ideas of holding annual professional conferences in the unlikely event of the new organisation ever being formed.

It was the end. I then put to the meeting the only main motion that day which came near to winning the unanimous votes of both sides.

It came from the Newcastle Branch of the NUJ . . . that, because of the evident fundamental and irreconcilable differences between the NUJ and IOJ, discussions of the merger proposals on the basis of the draft rules before this conference, be ended, and this conference be terminated forthwith.

The result of the separate counts of voters of both organisations showed a total of 250 in favour and only 7 against.

It was time to pack up all that paperwork and go, but first there were commiserations and sincere expressions of hope that much of the understanding and goodwill well founded between some members of both organisations during the 'trial marriage' might somehow be retained and nurtured.

That evening at a reception for the delegates, given by the Mayor of Southend at the Civic Centre, we held our final social fraternisation. There more genuine expressions of regret and wise hopes for the future co-operation of all journalists were again expressed.

It was the night the clocks went back, but I was perhaps too busy thinking of the future to remember to alter my watch. The next morning at an unusually early hour, long before breakfast, I walked as far as the pier enjoying the sunshine shimmering on the sea. It was a golden morning, brilliantly inspiring. It seemed a good omen then, but looking back I know my new optimism really stemmed from the realisation that many good friends in the Institute were suddenly back together, and once more on the same side sharing the same purpose.

At last we knew where we stood. The path ahead was littered with obstacles, some formidable, but the horizon was clear. Suddenly we had a goal in sight for which we could all strive without delay. The urgency was to surmount those difficulties, some real and some imaginary, which stood between us and our return to our full function, particularly in the trade union field. The credibility of the Institute and our future recruitment depended on it.

In the next few weeks the General Secretary, Bob Farmer, and his deputy Jim Paterson, and our small headquarters staff hardly paused in their efforts. The frequency of meetings at Tudor Street actually increased, but the whole direction of our deliberations had changed. Such consultations, even the most tedious of them became a joy if only for the pleasure of mentally ticking off the progress we were making on the way back. It was a great inspiration also to witness at first hand the determined resurgent spirit of old and young members.

In the next three months of my Presidency – whilst we still maintained a liaison committee with the NUJ – the cheerful, purposeful spirit prevailed and grew as we disengaged from the negotiations of those long years and secured our future. The news from the Districts was especially encouraging.

Most Presidential years are challenging. If mine was particularly so it confirmed for me, and for many others that the Institute thrives best when its members see it under threat or facing a crisis. From that point of view the year 1971 to 1972 was certainly invigorating, but I had a special asset. My wife, Nancy, was a member in her own right and needed no prompting in IOJ affairs. She worked assiduously and most encouragingly. Without her it would have been hard going indeed.

When we handed over the symbols of office to Henry and Elizabeth Douglas, we shared the same happy confidence, now so well proven by events. We knew the Institute of Journalists had enough old and new friends to replenish its creative enthusiasm, and sufficient wise architects to restore its strength and shape its future.

To restore the Institute to its full independence, to regain its former high reputation in Salaries and Conditions negotiations, and to reinstate other functions which had, by solemn agreement with the NUJ, fallen into abeyance, was of the utmost urgency.

On the least cautious estimate it could have taken years and that would have been too late. The Institute had only months to build up a new head of steam. It was achieved with remarkable speed and success through the spontaneous and unremitting efforts of many members guided mainly by the wisdom of a reunited Council, its Executive Committee and an enthusiastic, overworked headquarters staff. The skill and advice of the General Secretary was a major contribution to the rapid transition.

By New Year's Eve, 1972, the plans had been laid and hopes were high for the expansion and extension of activities which quickly transpired.

All these attempts at creating one organisation of journalists have been bedevilled by the very diversity of journalism and journalists: it is this situation which has created two divergent conceptions of the role of an organisation for journalists and two organisations through which, in their respective approaches, they seek to achieve the same fundamental aims.

It is paradoxical that within each organisation of journalists there are substantial numbers of the membership who support the aims and objects of the other. There are within both organisations those who strongly believe in journalism as a profession, though there are no qualifying examinations similar to those of other ancient professions, and on the other hand there are those in both unions who believe in the conventional trade union role and approach.

Subsequent developments within the NUJ, notably the left-ward political lurch of its leadership over several years, and its closed shop policy, have demonstrated the practical necessity for two separate organisations.

It is the closed shop policy perhaps more than any other factor that has disclosed the need for an alternative organisation if the journalists' liberty and freedom to carry on his or her chosen career is to be maintained.

FREELANCES

The advantages of Institute membership were more apparent to staff journalists than to freelances, who generally provided feature material and negotiated their terms direct with individual editors. The growth in newspapers in the early years of the present century had opened up markets for the freelance, for whom it was in the nature of a golden era. Many, however, joined the Institute for the status it afforded them.

The 1914–18 war brought an end to this profitable market. Sizes of newspapers were restricted: there was no room for their contributions, except the famous few. After the war, there was a flood of new entrants to the newspaper world and staff jobs were hard to come by for many years. Many tried freelance journalism after being lured by the schools of journalism which mushroomed and exploited the situation. Between the wars British journalism was a barren land for the freelance.

With the outbreak of war again in 1939 the situation repeated itself: markets vanished as newsprint rationing reduced papers to a fraction of their normal size.

Past experience had shown the need for planning and mid-way through the war a start was made to ascertain future opportunities and requirements.

Throughout the Institute's history freelances had occupied a back seat in its discussions and activities compared with the involvement of staff journalists. They had no representation on the council although they numbered about 600 of the Institute's total membership.

Colonel Reginald Lester, who had been a regular contributor to national and technical journals and the author of a number of books, was one who thought freelances had had a bad deal and, at the annual general meeting in 1943, he successfully advocated the formation of a separate section for freelances and became the first chairman when the plan came to fruition the following year. In 1957 he had the distinction of becoming the first freelance to be elected President of the Institute.

His promise that if a freelance section were formed it would be one of the most virile of the Institute sections has been upheld: it is now the largest of the divisions.

WOMEN IN JOURNALISM

Discussing how the status of women journalists had increased, R. D. Blumenfeld once recalled that when he first arrived in Fleet Street in 1900 there were only two women journalists there: thirty years later every newspaper had at least one woman on its staff.

There had been women proprietors: the *Sunday Times* had had two – Alice Cornwell, who was born in Essex and made a fortune from gold mining in Australia (she was nicknamed Princess Midas), bought it in 1887 and was succeeded as proprietor in 1893 by another woman, Mrs Rachel Beer, the aunt of Siegfried Sassoon. And Lady Bathurst, Lord Glenesk's daughter, had inherited the *Morning Post*. Of women journalists one of the most distinguished of the early practitioners was Flora Shaw who, in the 1890s, became the first professional woman staff correspondent and Colonial Editor of *The Times*.

Within the Institute women journalists had taken a prominent role. One of these was Miss Catherine Drew, to whom the council presented a gold bracelet in 1908 on her retirement from active journalism in gratitude of her services to the Institute. She was one of the small number of respected women journalists whose names appeared on the first enrolment of the corporate body and was the first woman to be elected a Vice President and a councillor. On her death two years later Miss Drew bequeathed the bracelet to the Institute with the express desire that it should pass to the keeping each year of the President's wife or the lady assisting him in his presidential duties. It has been worn by successive president's ladies ever since, thus perpetuating the name of this Institute pioneer.

During the suffragette campaign, women journalists were particularly suspect and were excluded from the Central Criminal

Court after there had been angry scenes in the public galleries at the trial of Mrs Pankhurst. The scenes, it was recorded, would undoubtedly militate against the admission of women to future trials of militant suffragists and the Institute exercised vigilance to see that any future exclusions did not apply to women journalists who were there to pursue their profession. The clerk of the Court, when tackled by the Institute, replied that properly accredited women journalists would be allowed to remain in court at all times unless the proceedings had to be conducted *in camera*.

In the latter part of the nineteenth century journalism was one of the few occupations that were available to women, but the spread of education and the growth of professionalism created conditions for them to operate as equals with their male colleagues.

Given that women members had played a leading part in its affairs from the start it is surprising that the Institute has so far had only one woman president. That distinction is held by Miss Marguerite Peacocke, a freelance and a member of London District, who occupied the presidency in 1967.

At that time she had worked in Fleet Street for more than thirty years: she has recalled the scene in which many women freelances operated in the 1930s:

There was a community of women freelances, all regular contributors to the national dailies, London evenings and the major provincials, who gathered at church doors, in theatre foyers and at the entrances to private views and parties, noting the names of arrivals with details of hats and dresses and watching for any face which would make it worth while putting in an extra 'black' for some local weekly.

Some came from aristocratic or high ranking service families which had fallen on hard times. With no newspaper office experience, an almost comically amateurish style of writing, and a very limited news sense, they chose this field of journalism as a means of turning to account their only assets – a wide circle of well-connected aquaintances, an inbred grasp of the niceties of etiquette, an encyclopaedic knowledge of top family trees, and a quick accurate eye for identifying uniforms, decorations and insignia of rank.

Demand had dwindled for the old 'Ins and Outs' at 2s 6d a time – 'The Duchess of Blank has arrived at her London residence', 'The Duke of Dash has left for the Riviera', but the society market was no longer limited to Court paragraphs. 'Diary' editors took copy and even news editors who sent reporters to society functions would often rely on the expert contributor for an accurate list of names.

In its own way this was a highly expert job.

One was expected to know by sight every duchess and her grown-up daughters and daughters-in-law, all the other socially active peeresses, wives of all members of the Government, ambassadors and ministers, anyone connected with the royal households, and a number of society personalities. The menfolk one identified by their presence with their wives or family parties.

One had to get down names and dress details as guests walked past, and was plagued by social climbers interrupting that they were Mrs John Brown, Smith or Robinson and refusing to move until this was recorded. And the round of calls at houses and embassies had to begin before 9 a.m. to catch the early risers, and did not end until one caught the last ones as they returned to dress for dinner. And in between were christenings, weddings, luncheons, teas and cocktail parties, and the theatre first nights following, with the coming-out dances and charity balls which did not start till shortly before midnight. There would be three or even four visits to Fleet Street to fit in to deliver copy. In self-defence one developed a near miraculous memory for voices as well as faces, good feet, and the ability to go without food or to swallow odds and ends from one's handbag without being detected.

Everyone who was anyone knew the society journalists and regarded them as being at least as important as their editors, and Queen Mary always acknowledged their curtseys with a smile and a pause to enable them to take in the details of her dress and note who was in attendance on her. Other royalties took their cue from her and when some officious host tried occasionally to relegate them to some corner where observation was difficult, they would deliberately walk that way to give the journalists a close-up view.

The advent of the gossip column in popular newspapers, recording the more personal activities of public figures, brought an extension of the social reporter role of many women journalists.

Reporting developments in the fashion world for the growing female readership of newspapers and magazines was a natural consequence and gradually they took their place in the former strongholds of male journalists, throwing off the discriminatory 'lady journalist' descriptions of the pioneers.

The effects of two world wars, the increasing interest of female readers and the establishment of papers and magazines especially for women encouraged their wider role and acceptance of equality in journalistic flair, ability and opportunity.

Today women journalists occupy important executive positions, while others have become popular columnists in the general features area of newspapers: no distinctions are drawn – as reporters they cover every kind of story and diary engagement; others, as sub-editors, have mastered the intricacies of headline writing and page make-up; all work the necessarily irregular and unsocial hours that production of a newspaper or a news broadcast demands.

11 The Post-War Newspaper Industry

For some time after the end of the Second World War the number of pages continued to be limited because of continuing newsprint rationing due to import restrictions. In fact, the restrictions were not finally relaxed until 1956, eleven years after the ending of the war, when competition returned and the more successful papers were able to give better value to their readers than their weaker rivals.

An economic recession in 1951 resulted in a general increase in the cover price of newspapers. Before that increase the aggregate sale of daily national newspapers had reached a peak of over 16.5 million copies a day. The price increase had some effect on sales, but three years later sales had peaked again. But provincial newspapers were less fortunate in re-establishing circulation and sales dropped by 17 per cent.

Trends in newspaper reading fluctuated. No doubt as a result of the war the favourite newspapers in the 1950s were those which had an emphasis towards strip cartoons, pictures and human interest features, but in the case of Sunday newspapers an opposite trend was evident, with the so-called quality papers advancing their circulations. There was no doubt a social reason: the decline of church attendance meant a greater accent on leisure weekends, with more time devoted to reading the papers.

There was little inclination in the post-war years to start up new newspapers: indeed the trend was much the reverse. Those new births that did appear had a short and chequered life. Mr W. J. Brittain in October 1953 launched the first new daily paper for forty-one years (apart from the Communist *Daily Worker*). But it failed to attract sufficient of the serious readership at which it was aimed and ceased publication after only five months.

Seven years later *The New Daily* – 'the only daily newspaper in Great Britain independent of combines and trade unions' – made its appearance, run by a committee headed by Mr Edward Martell. It too had a relatively short life, changing its format early in 1965 from a general newspaper to a commentary in magazine form on current affairs from the radical right viewpoint.

Taking advantage of the increasing readership of quality papers, the *Sunday Telegraph* was launched in July 1960, the first Sunday paper since the launching of the *Sunday Express* by Lord Beaverbrook forty years earlier.

It was an unpropitious time for newspapers. In the late 1950s there had been much speculation about the future of two national dailies, the *News Chronicle* and the *Daily Herald*, which was jointly owned by Odhams Press and the TUC, including rumours of a merger of the two. In the event the *News Chronicle* struggled on while an agreement was later reached under which Odhams secured editorial freedom and a licence to print the *Herald*, with a pledge to support the TUC and the Labour Party.

The economics of newspaper production lost none of their harshness and the roundabout of increased cover prices to offset the high cost of newsprint continued, with casualties falling both nationally and locally. Some old established provincial news-papers like the *Yorkshire Observer*, with over 120 years of history, disappeared while the *Birmingham Gazette*, which had been founded in 1741, was merged with the *Birmingham Post*.

Nationally, the years of 1960–61 were the most disastrous in the history of journalism, with five major national papers disappear-ing: the *News Chronicle* finally succumbed and was merged with the *Daily Mail*; its stable-mate *The Star* went with it, merging with the *London Evening News*; the *Sunday Graphic* closed after forty-five years of publication; the *Sunday Dispatch* was absorbed by the *Sunday Express*; and the *Empire News* was merged with the *News of the World*. Their combined circulations were in excess of 6 million.

It was difficult to appreciate that newspapers with large circulations could be uneconomic: the *News Chronicle*, for instance, had a circulation of over one million copies daily, the *Empire News* sold over 2 million and the *Sunday Dispatch* nearly 1.5 million. But production costs had risen in a spectacular way and newspapers that were unable to exist on their own profits had to go out of business altogether or either form an association with a large publishing group or find some wholly different business that would sustain it from its more diverse profits.

Around the same time the *Daily Mirror* group made a successful take-over of Odhams Press, thus creating the largest newspaper and magazine publishing group in Britain.

All these developments gave rise to public unease and there was also much concern within the industry itself about the dangers of the increasing concentration of ownership and about the future of the industry.

The 1960s had started off badly for the national Press; the provincial press was not to escape the harsh economic realities that had decimated their national colleagues. Their blackest year came in 1963/64 when five evening newspapers disappeared: the *Nottingham Evening News* merged with the *Nottingham Evening Post*; the *Manchester Evening Chronicle* with the *Manchester Evening News*; the *Yorkshire Evening News* with the rival *Yorkshire Evening Post*; the *Leicester Evening Mail* with the *Leicester Mercury*; and the *Edinburgh Evening Dispatch* with the *Edinburgh Evening News*. There were also heavy losses in the local paper field. Meanwhile there were further instances of a concentration of ownership in large groups.

One of the recommendations of the 1962 Royal Commission on the Press which, under the chairmanship of Lord Shawcross, had been instructed to examine the economic and financial factors affecting newspaper and periodical publication, was the setting up of a Press Amalgamations Court. The continuing trend towards concentration of ownership led the Labour Government in 1965 to introduce a Monopolies and Mergers Bill with the object of setting up a commission to investigate mergers generally. Significantly, the first case to come before it involved newspapers: the amalgamation of *The Times* and the *Sunday Times* by Lord Thomson.

The trend was to continue. At the beginning of 1969 Mr Rupert Murdoch won control of the *News of the World*, which had been in the Carr family since 1891. Sir Emsley Carr, a former president of the Institute, was its editor for a remarkable fifty years' span. Mr Murdoch extended his British newspaper interests by acquiring *The Sun* from IPC. He relaunched it in a new style in November 1969, emulating and competing with the *Daily Mirror*.

Meanwhile there were further casualties through rising costs and falling advertising. The *Daily Sketch* was the next to fall in May 1971 when it was merged with a restyled tabloid-sized *Daily Mail*.

The 1970s was also a dark decade. The 1962 Royal Commission had diagnosed one of the most serious threats to the industry:

overmanning on the production side of newspapers coupled with a variety of restrictive practices and a resistance to the introduction of modern labour-saving techniques which were being adopted elsewhere in the world and, indeed, to some extent in provincial newspapers.

Lord Shawcross, who chaired the 1962 inquiry and subsequently became chairman of the Press Council, commented in the Council's annual report for 1973–74: 'Although the illness had been correctly diagnosed and appropriate remedies prescribed, the patient could not be induced to take the medicine.'

The causes of the illness continued unchecked and were exacerbated by the high cost of newsprint and increasing competition for advertising, particularly from television and from radio, after the passage of the Sound Broadcasting Bill had permitted the introduction of commercial radio.

It was not surprising that the announcement of the setting up of yet another Royal Commission in 1973, the third to inquire into the state of the Press since the ending of the Second World War, met with little enthusiasm either in Parliament or in the national Press.

Mr Edward Heath, then Leader of the Opposition, summed up the general feeling when he said all those concerned with the Press knew very well what the problems were: what was needed was action largely within the industry to put its own house in order. In his own words:

All the information about the Press is available. The recommendations of previous Royal Commissions are worth rereading. Nothing has basically changed in the situation except that we are now twelve years further out of date in reorganisation of the industry and just as far as ever from achieving a settlement of the basic problems. The first underlying basic problem of national newspapers in Fleet Street is out-of-date plant and machinery. Another is the gross overmanning of existing plant and overmanning even when new plant is being installed. The third is the weakness of management in not unifying to handle reinvestment of the industry and overmanning.

Few would argue with his summary even after a further decade.

As the decade drew to a close, Fleet Street in particular was further bedevilled by industrial problems which resulted in lost sales of both national dailies and Sunday papers which, in 1978 alone, were estimated at 155 million copies.

That year ended with the suspension of *The Times* and *Sunday Times* when management failed to reach agreement with the various unions on procedures to overcome the frequent disputes and interruption of production and on the introduction of new technology. The suspension of publication lasted eleven months. Throughout that period journalists had been kept on full pay: many diverted their energies to authorship. The suspension cost Times Newspapers Ltd an estimated £40 million and the final settlement failed to achieve all the company's objectives: indeed some of those that were agreed did not operate. The company was being heavily subsidised by the parent company, Thomson British Holdings, and disruption recurred. The final straw for Lord Thomson was a strike by NUJ journalists over a pay dispute: he regarded their action as a betrayal and in 1980 it was announced that the Thomson Organisation was withdrawing from publication of the papers and its supplements and was trying to sell them.

An offer from Mr Rupert Murdoch's News International group, owners of *The Sun* and *News of the World*, was accepted: the transfer of ownership was accepted by the Government without reference to the Monopolies Commission. New manning levels were agreed with the new owner over a hectic three-week period of negotiations. They included an agreement on electronic photo-composition. Although *The Times* was the first Fleet Street newspaper to be wholly set by new technology, the objective of single keystroking – direct access to the computer-based typesetting system by journalists and tele-sales staff – remains to be achieved.

With the change of ownership came a change of editor. Mr Harold Evans, whose editorship of the *Sunday Times* since 1967 had earned him a high reputation as a campaigning journalist, was appointed. His conduct of a series of investigations had brought him international renown. He was a member of the Institute and his campaign on behalf of thalidomide children, an outstanding stand in defence of Press freedom, earned him the award of the Institute's coveted Gold Medal.

Mr Evans's rule was, however, a brief one. After a year and a series of differences with Mr Murdoch, which have been documented by Mr Evans in his book *Good Times, Bad Times*,

(Weidenfeld and Nicolson, 1983) the Chairman sought his resignation.

The proposed sale of the *Observer* in 1981 to George Outram and Co., a subsidiary of Lonrho, was referred to the Monopolies and Mergers Commission. In its comment to the Commission, the Institute did not think the merger raised important issues of concentration of ownership, since the Outram morning and evening newspapers, together with a new 'quality' Sunday paper launched in April of that year (which, incidentally, ceased publication in 1983) were confined almost entirely to Scotland. But it did enter a reservation over possible conflict with Lonhro's widespread overseas interests.

> Initially, no doubt, the company would be content to exploit the kudos that proprietorship of the *Observer* would bring. But we believe that sooner or later the exercise of genuine editorial independence by the newspaper would be thought by the company to be harmful to its interests when dealing with people in countries where the concept of such independence is little understood and even less respected.

How percipient was the Institute in its view was to be evidenced in April 1984 when there was an astonishing dispute between the editor of the *Observer*, Mr Donald Trelford, and the chairman of Lonrho and the *Observer*, Mr Tiny Rowland. An article by Mr Trelford following a visit to Zimbabwe, alleged atrocities by Zimbabwean troops in Matabeleland: it was immediately dis-owned by Mr Rowland in a letter to Mr Robert Mugabe, the Prime Minister, in which he apologised for its publication. Mr Rowland was in turn censured by the newspaper's independent directors for improper proprietorial interference in editorial freedom. His public criticism of the editor constituted an inhibition, if not a restraint, on the editor's freedom, they said.

After rumbling along for several days the dispute was resolved and the tetchy relationship of the two main participants patched up, but it did provide a salutory lesson in the preservation of editorial independence and illustrated how right the Institute had been in drawing attention to the potential threat inherent in the acquisition of a leading newspaper by an international company with widespread interests outside newspapers.

ADMISSION OF THE PRESS

Relations between the Press and local councils and other public authorities had been a matter of continuing difficulty over many years. It was one of the problems with which the Institute had had to deal in its infancy.

The question of the right of attendance at meetings of local authorities was at issue: in the opinion of newspapers too much public business was conducted in private to the detriment of the interests of ratepayers.

In 1907 Mr Frank Mason, editor-proprietor of the *Tenby Observer* was banned from meetings of the local council because the councillors were outraged by his report of their meeting. He took the issue to the High Court which gave the astonishing ruling that council meetings were private.

Although Mason lost his case, the ensuing controversy resulted in the passing of the Admission of the Press Act the following year. Mason's battle is commemorated modestly on a plaque outside the Tenby newspaper office which reads: 'The Tenby Observer. Established 1853. A pioneer of Press freedom.'

Radical changes occurred in the years after the enactment of that legislation, with many new-style public authorities coming into existence. Some were elected, others were not but all were spending public money and the interests of ratepayers and taxpayers needed to be safeguarded through the reporting of the activities of these bodies.

The proposed amendment of the 1908 Act to meet the changed situation was frequently discussed by newspaper organisations and in the early 1950s a sub-committee of all the organisations concerned – the Newspaper Publishers' Association, Newspaper Society, Institute of Journalists, National Union of Journalists, Press Association and Guild of Editors – drew up amendments to secure the right to more freely report the proceedings of all authorities which spent public finance. Parliamentary progress was slow and it was not until 1956 that a new Bill was introduced. Even then it failed to complete all the parliamentary stages: then the Suez crisis arose and made its reintroduction impossible.

Another attempt was made the following year when there was discussion of new clauses reaffirming the basic principle that reporters should be admitted to meetings of all local authorities with the proviso that they could be excluded by resolution of the council when confidential matters were being discussed. As discussions were currently taking place between the Minister of Local Government and the local authority organisations, these clauses were withdrawn. However, a dispute in the printing industry in 1959 affecting local newspapers brought the matter to public attention again when a number of councils boycotted emergency editions of local papers and decided to withdraw information from them and to exclude the Press in such circumstances from their meetings.

That year a new and determined Member of Parliament was elected for the Finchley constituency in North London and a few months later when that new MP, Mrs Margaret Thatcher, was successful in the ballot for Private Members' Bills she took up the cause and made an early reputation for herself with a new Public Bodies (Admissions to Meetings) Bill, providing for the admission of Press representatives and members of the public to meetings of certain bodies exercising public functions. It afforded the Press the right to attend any committee meeting of a public body whose members consisted of or included all members of the body: it also stipulated that the Press must be supplied with copies of the agenda and other statements.

The Government approved the Bill in principle: thus action was taken at last against an irritant of many years' standing. It is ironic that reports of the proceedings of the House of Commons itself since 1762 had been an infringement of parliamentary privilege and it was not until 1968 that this iniquity was formally rescinded by a select commitee.

PRESS ETHICS

The 1947 Royal Commission on the Press took two years to produce its report in which, taking account of public concern about the effects of the declining number of newspapers and the deterioration of journalistic standards, it recommended the setting up of a General Council of the Press. The competition for mass circulations, it said, had produced a tendency to abandon values and encourage reliance on sensationalism and triviality.

The Press Council formally came into existence on 1 July 1953 with the aim of safeguarding the freedom of the Press and combatting its abuse. Its functions were to condemn any practices which could only bring the Press into disrepute, to investigate complaints and, where these were justified, to seek redress and to answer criticisms which were adjudged to be unfair or ill-founded. Its funding came from the constituent organisations of the newspaper industry. Major J. J. Astor (later Lord Astor of Hever), proprietor of *The Times* was its first chairman but he resigned after a year owing to illness and was succeeded by Sir Linton Andrews, editor of the *Yorkshire Post* and a former President of the Institute. He in turn was succeeded in 1959 by another Institute member, Mr George Murray of the *Daily Mail*. Mr Alan Pitt-Robbins, news editor of *The Times* was its secretary from the outset until 1960. They and their Institute successors have from its inception played a prominent part in the Council's discussions from which has been built up a considerable case law on matters of journalistic practice and principle.

In 1980 the NUJ left the Council claiming its rulings were slow and ineffectual, that it had done nothing to stem the continuing concentration of the Press, that it had not lifted journalistic ethical standards, that its funding was wrong, and it was indifferent to self-reform.

Since then it has been left to the Institute nominees, together with the Guild of Editors, to represent the working journalist. It has, in fact, reformed itself and met the wishes of the original Royal Commission and its successors by increasing the lay membership to equality with the professional representatives and by taking steps to speed up its process in dealing with complaints.

The more aggressive methods of news gathering undoubtedly generated considerable disfavour against the Press in the post-war years of the 1950s: the Council in its first annual report commented that much ill-feeling against the Press had been caused by the very natural resentment against intrusion into the private lives of individuals in cases where mere curiosity unrelated to public interest had led to callous methods of inquiry.

Some of the changes in journalistic approach were a reflection of the social and moral changes that had taken place during the first half of the century. Briton's of the 1950s and 1960s – 'Swinging Britain' as it became known – accepted without demur things that would have horrified their grandparents. Neverthe-less, as *The Times* observed: 'The race for mammoth circulations has led in some cases to a disgraceful lowering of values. The baser instincts are pandered to, not only in lasciviousness – the influence of this can be overrated – but in social attitudes and in conduct as well.'

Standards were to deteriorate even more, with nudity becoming commonplace in some of the tabloid popular papers. The reporting by some newspapers of the controversial obscenity trial in 1961, involving D. H. Lawrence's novel *Lady Chatterley's Lover*, illustrated the degree to which newspapers had moved: the trial turned on the use in the novel of four letter words, which were repeated in their reports of the trial by some newspapers, notably the *Guardian* (which by then had dropped the name of the city of its birth and moved its printing to London), the *Observer* and the weekly magazine, *Spectator*. The Press Council found the use of these words 'objectionable and unnecessary'. In general, it said, the Press had demonstrated how a court case of that kind could be adequately and broadmindedly reported without debasing standards of decency.

12 The Closed Shop Issue

Of the many matters to which journalists have had to devote their attention, none has aroused the ferocity and tension of the closed shop in journalism, particularly during the 1970s. It occupied many hours of debate inside and outside Parliament and provided columns of published letters to the editor; it resulted in the two longest-running strikes in the history of British journalism, as well as many smaller but no less unpleasant incidents: it set colleague against colleague and saw the use of unbecoming and unprofessional tactics in blatant attempts at coercion.

Journalists accustomed to reporting the dramas of others found themselves at the heart of an issue that deeply affected them personally and one in which their future careers in many instances were at stake.

The closed shop was an established fact in many industries, including printing and the production side of newspapers. Up to 1971 when the then Conservative Government's Industrial Relations Act was introduced, closed shops had been legal and, indeed, frequently agreed on the initiative of managements on the grounds, it was claimed, that they helped to stabilise industrial relations and avoided inter-union disputes.

In newspapers where there were a multiplicity of print unions, they formed part of the familiar pattern of appeasement by managements which has characterised the industry, particularly in Fleet Street, for many years.

In general industry there had been a rapid increase in the number of closed shops, especially in white-collar and other non-traditional areas in the 1960s which had caused public concern. It resulted in the 1971 legislation, which gave an employee the right to refuse 'on any reasonable grounds' to be a member of a particular trade union and also allowed a worker to belong to another 'appropriate' union.

When Labour was returned to power in 1974, Mr Michael Foot, a member of the NUJ, a former editor of the *Evening Standard*, and a journalist known for his libertarian instincts, became Secretary of State for Employment and introduced legislation seeking a return to the pre-1971 situation.

Whatever the arguments in favour and against closed shops elsewhere, their application to journalism raises fundamental issues of liberty and Press freedom. Consequently, closed shops in journalism were rare. In the limited number of instances where they had been negotiated, they were in the form of the post-entry variety and allowed existing members of other unions to retain that membership.

The NUJ had first sought post-entry closed shops as early as 1920 but the campaigns had been intermittent, usually renewed with a little more vigour after each merger failure. 'It is difficult to imagine anything more horrible than a closed shop for news and comment,' declared Mr Gordon Robbins who, because of the war, served a double term as President, in his 1943 presidential address. 'It would be a gross violation of that freedom of the Press which is one of the war aims. The Institute can never compromise on the closed shop issue.'

The IOJ had just been recognised by the Newspaper Publishers' Association as a negotiating and signatory party on agreements on salaries and conditions, a recognition which was soon afterwards also accorded by the Newspaper Society. The action infuriated the NUJ who, not unnaturally, intensified their closed shop agitation.

A new generation was beginning to adopt tougher measures in the campaign: journalists were coerced into resigning from the Institute on taking up new appointments.

Many NUJ chapels, while accepting that 100 per cent membership was desirable, creditably declined to bring it about by threats, intimidation and coercion. Nor was there overwhelming enthusiasm to go on strike in its pursuit. When an Institute member resisted attempts to persuade him to join the Union when he joined the *Birmingham Post* in 1951, the resultant demand by the NUJ chapel for a closed shop was, in line with Newspaper Society policy, rejected by the management and the union chapel became split over a call for strike action if the closed shop principle was not applied.

It was in the 1970s, however, that the agitation became a fervour for a variety of reasons. Before discussing that era it is helpful to consider the atmosphere of the period and look at it in its proper perspective.

The previous decade in Britain had seen a period of educational upheaval, with students taking part in sit-ins and occupation of university administrative buildings in protest at a variety of alleged grievances. It is beyond question that many of the graduates who had participated in these disturbances and, if not actually serving a political apprenticeship through them, had certainly had their political awareness and passions aroused in that extraordinary educational environment, later found their way into journalism, along with others who undoubtedly had political motivation and saw journalism as a means of furthering their political aspirations.

Educational reforms of earlier years were also having an effect. More universities had been created to accommodate the growing army of students, and the employment market consequently had many more graduates to cope with.

Methods of recruitment to industry were changing and journalism was no exception. While the traditional form of recruitment of school leavers by local newspapers remained one method of entry, there was increased recruitment of graduates: many of the larger provincial newspaper groups now operated graduate entry schemes through which suitable candidates were recruited in the universities and offered posts on graduation.

Left-wing infiltration of the NUJ had begun some time before and by the early 1970s far-left groups like International Socialists were active. It was the classic situation: traditionally branch meetings had provided for those who took an interest in union affairs a social occasion after the necessary business had been completed – for many, assistance with organising the local press ball in aid of charities was the limit of their involvement in union affairs. The majority of ordinary members were content to get on with their job and leave the running of the organisation to other more willing members.

Attitudes were also changing. It was not only members of the IOJ who regarded journalism as a respected profession: an older generation of Union members had similar ideas on the vocational nature of their calling, of the need to provide a service to their paper's readers. They were apathetic to Union activities but were being joined by a new generation more politically expressive and envious of the tight grip of the print unions whose example they would have liked to emulate. It was a situation ripe for exploitation by extremists and one of which they took full advantage.

The breakdown of the latest round of merger talks was another factor in the picture: it resulted in the customary revival of closed shop agitation.

There the matter might have gently simmered had not public attention been focussed upon it by Mr Foot's activities in Westminster. His attempt to return to the pre-1971 position coincided not only with boastful expressions in the NUJ's official newspaper that militants were now in control and that a nationalised Press under workers' control was the panacea for all the ills of the media but with two decisions of the Union conference: reaffirmation but in stronger terms than usual that all journalistic work should be the monopoly of NUJ members and that editors who had hitherto enjoyed special status as associate members must now become full members and, as such, would be subject to the discipline of the Union. This latter move backfired to a large extent when many editors resigned their membership, although resignation would not have provided an escape route for editors had Mr Foot's original intentions ever been implemented.

The early parliamentary moves were the start of an eighteen-month long clash of principles and personalities that provided days and nights of drama, especially as it was also a period of minority Government when an alliance of Opposition and Liberal MPs could put the Government in serious difficulties.

As if Mr Foot's proposals were not sufficient to create a furore, evidence was coincidentally emerging of the 'blacking' of editorial copy written by non-NUJ members.

At the *Kentish Times* series of newspapers the boycott had been applied to articles written by district editors, while at the *Birmingham Post* wire room and printing operatives acceded to an NUJ request not to handle articles by the paper's London based economics correspondent, Ian Richardson, a member of the IOJ, to which the management and the then editor, Mr David Hopkinson, responded by refusing to produce the paper without Mr Richardson's articles.

Ostensibly the 'blacking' was claimed to be a temporary sanction which would be removed immediately a current pay dispute was settled, but incidents of this kind alongside the proposed legislation drew public interest to the issues at a crucial stage of the debate and served to focus attention on the dangers to Press freedom inherent in a journalistic closed shop.

In the political straitjacket in which the Labour Government found itself there was little room for manoeuvre and Mr Foot was faced with a combination of Opposition and Liberal forces defeating his objects in the House of Commons and a House of Lords even more opposed to his proposals and making further changes. His tactic was to introduce a short Amending Bill to remove provisions and safeguards written into the Act by Opposition MPs and peers against the Government's wishes and to restore the clauses that would lead to the approval of a closed shop in the media.

In the subsequent debates Mr Foot argued that his Bill was permissive rather than coercive and denied that, if enacted, it would give a signal and encourage wholesale demands for closed shops.

Outside Parliament, the IOJ was prominent among opponents of the measures who included the International Press Institute and a spontaneous grouping of editors who sent a deputation to see Mr Foot and produced a pamphlet, written by Mr David Astor (then editor of the *Observer*), Sir Denis Hamilton (then editor in chief of Times Newspapers) and Mr Alastair Hetherington (then editor of the *Guardian*). In it they explained the dangers to freedom of expression that could flow from Mr Foot's Bill unless newspapers and broadcasting were exempt from its provisions. This unusual combination of editors prompted Harold Evans, then editor of the *Sunday Times*, to observe that Fleet Street editors usually spent their competitive lives trying to do each other down and were afraid to be seen to agree on the time of day for fear of jeopardising their independence.

The Press Council had earlier been asked to consider the operation of the closed shop in journalism as being an unprofessional activity and a direct threat to the freedom of the Press which the Council existed to defend. It declined to pronounce publicly at that time but later referred to the subject in its evidence to the Royal Commission on the Press, which was at that time sitting. The Council strongly condemned a closed shop in newspapers and magazines, preventing contributions from people not belonging to a particular union. 'The Council would regard this as a totally unacceptable assault upon freedom of expression', it said. The operation of an imposed code would be a serious threat to Press freedom and, with the benefit of nearly a quarter of a century's experience of newspaper ethics, it believed that neither wit nor ingenuity could produce a code adequate to cover the apparently infinite variations in ethical situations.

In its own evidence to the Royal Commission, the Institute declared its total opposition to a single union for journalists. It pointed out that at that time a journalist might disobey union instructions to act in a manner contrary to professional conscience secure in the knowledge that if he were expelled he may either join the alternative union or remain outside both without risk of being dismissed, but in a single-union closed shop situation the journalist would not only court dismissal: he could also face the prospect of being unable to find work elsewhere.

The power of the union would be immense and give rise to the danger of the use of that power to impose a single policy in regard to certain aspects of editorial selection and treatment on all publications. The muted and one-sided reporting that would result from a closed shop would be a major threat to the diversity and independence of the Press that could be equalled only by stringent Government censorship.

Mr Foot's proposals were going through the parliamentary procedures and being knocked about by amendments in both Houses. In the House of Lords, Lord Goodman emerged as the crusading hero. The position of editors was one of the crucial issues: another was how to safeguard Press freedom. On the latter Lord Houghton had suggested a voluntary charter of Press freedoms to be annexed to Mr Foot's Bill as a code of practice, with the Minister drafting and imposing a charter if voluntary agreement was not reached.

Lord Goodman, who was then chairman of the Newspaper Publishers' Association, accepted the idea of a voluntary charter and had an amendment inserted giving journalists four basic rights under the charter. Under his proposals, editors would be under no obligation to join a union and would have the right to commission, publish or not publish any article free from pressure by industrial action; journalists, including editors, would have the right to join the union of their choice and would also have the right not to be arbitrarily or unreasonably expelled from union membership.

His clause on union membership was specifically to ensure that the Institute was not eliminated by the NUJ. His proposals met with a generally favourable reaction, with the exception of hardliners within the NUJ.

The NUJ had supported Lord Houghton's idea of a Press charter and had offered exemption to editors where a post-entry closed shop had been obtained. At the 1975 delegates' meeting, however, hardliners triumphed and, against the advice of Mr Kenneth Morgan, then general secretary, and other moderates not to jeopardise the Houghton proposal, committed the Union to a militant line on closed shops and the role of editors. The Union executive's earlier decision to exempt editors was reversed and other resolutions opposed any charter on Press freedom and declared a policy of 100 per cent post-entry membership in all future national and house agreements.

The events showed the disunity that existed in the ranks of the Union and had the effect of strengthening support for Lord Goodman's proposals. Moderates within the Union pledged themselves to reverse the decisions and in the succeeding weeks campaigned against the hardline policy and secured a ballot of members on the issues. In this they had some success, overthrowing the ruling on editors but support for the goal of 100 per cent membership remained, although the size of the majority indicated deep hostility to the whole concept of the closed shop by many members.

The Westminster battle ended when Mr Foot's Bill was passed in March 1976: there then began a series of meetings to try to reach agreement on a voluntary code of practice – otherwise known as the charter. The period in which agreement was to be reached had been extended from six months to a year: if no agreement was reached by the parties taking part in the discussions, the Minister would produce his own charter.

The legislation resulted in a number of applications for closed shop agreements being submitted to provincial newspaper managements. Objections of the Newspaper Society to the issue remained unchanged: their members were advised to delay entering into any talks on the subject while discussions were taking place at the national level on the proposed Press charter.

The Union's pro-closed shop policy, now given added stimulus by the new legislation, had – as has been seen – created serious differences of opinion and divisions among journalists. The atmosphere became more tense in May 1976 when the Institute was granted a certificate of independence giving it legal status as a trade union under the Employment Protection Act.

Meanwhile incidents were occurring which provided timely examples of the dangers inherent in closed shops and the necessity for safeguards to protect journalists' freedoms and Press freedom in general.

An early example of this occurred at Barnsley where differences of opinion on the issue among the staff of the 120-year-old weekly *Barnsley Chronicle* resulted in four members of the staff, three of them long-standing NUJ members, deciding to transfer to the Institute. They were ostracised by their colleagues and the local NUJ branch urged the controlling Labour group on Barnsley Council and other news sources not to co-operate with them.

The request caused some embarrassment to the council, since it opened its committee meetings to the public: one of the journalists concerned covered labour stories and the fact that he was well respected in those circles did not make the situation any less ironic. Three of the rebels were sub-editors and it did not, of course, escape attention that their defection could render any future strike of journalists at the paper less effective.

There were similar incidents elsewhere: they focussed public attention on the issues that were under discussion in the charter talks. The Prime Minister, Mr Harold Wilson, disapproved of them and Mr Foot sought to get the Union to reconsider the dispute.

The first major strike over the closed shop took place in 1977 at Kettering in Northamptonshire: it was significant also because during its course attempts were made to involve the journalistic staff at the Press Association who had always held aloof of involvement in disputes at any of their subscribers because of their tradition of impartiality.

The NUJ chapel called the strike when the management of Northamptonshire Newspapers, part of the East Midland Allied Press Group refused to incorporate the closed shop principle in a new house agreement. 'We cannot have the input of news controlled by one union. There are two unions in journalism and we are not prepared to negotiate any clauses to a house agreement giving the NUJ a closed shop', said the editor of the *Northamptonshire Evening Telegraph*, Mr Ronald Hunt.

Support among Union members for a strike was not unanimous and nine members left to join the Institute. They found themselves caught in a net. A union rule that no member could resign while subject to disciplinary proceedings had been extended to prevent resignation during a stoppage.

Throughout the stoppage, the editor of the evening newspaper, Mr Hunt, produced a slimmed down version of his paper single handed. Part of the material he used emanated from the Press Association and some members of the NUJ at the PA wanted the teleprinted copy to be marked 'Not for Northants Evening Telegraph'. The editor-in-chief, Mr David Chipp, refused.

Some weeks later another attempt to involve the PA was made, when the NUJ executive ordered its members there to stop supplying copy and photographs where official disputes were in progress. This instruction resulted in a split among the members in the PA, who demanded that any instruction by the executive must be approved by a majority of all Union members at the agency. It was followed by the calling of a 24-hour strike to coincide with the announcement of local government election results.

The PA management had always taken the line of non-involvement in other people's disputes. Many of the Union members shared the management view that to give support to NUJ members involved in outside disputes would undermine the agency's independence, impartiality and integrity. They voted by 100 to 65 against the strike call; although the dissenters did stop work, the agency's service was totally unaffected.

The strike call was far from fully supported. All the provincial morning and evening newspapers appeared as usual and in Fleet Street NUJ members rejected or ignored an instruction to 'black' PA news copy and photographs.

The Kettering strike evaded settlement or compromise despite many interventions and formulae for twenty-four weeks. Eventually, on the intervention of the TUC print committee chairman, Mr W. Keys, general secretary of the Society of Graphical and Allied Trades, as intermediary, an uneasy compromise was reached. The nine defectors agreed to submit to disciplinary procedures which were to be completed by the end of August, after which they would decide their future membership.

They were given verbal assurances that if they resigned they would not be caught up in a closed shop move. They appeared before a special Union complaints hearing at the beginning of August and all were fined. The following November eight of the

nine original defectors announced their decision to leave the
Union but the following day retracted their resignations in return
for the withdrawal of demands for a post-entry closed shop or 100
per cent membership of the Union to be written into a new house
agreement. By their action they averted the resumption of a
further protracted strike and sacrificed their own freedom to
transfer so as to leave the door open for others to do so.

Three weeks after the fragile formula at Kettering, the NUJ
went into combat against one of the largest groups of provincial
newspapers in the country, Westminster Press, with over a
hundred daily and weekly papers in its ownership. The new
battleground was at Darlington.

The NUJ chapel there had the previous year unilaterally
declared that there should be a post-entry 100 per cent membership arrangement and several new recruits in the north-east
offices had yielded to heavy pressure to join the Union. One who
refused, however, was Mrs Josephine Kirk Smith, who had been
engaged as a sub-editor on the *Darlington and Stockton Times*.
Within two days of starting work there a Union member had
asked her whether she was a member of the Union. Within a week
she had been asked about her position by a Union official. She told
him she had formerly been a Union member but was considering
her position. She said that he replied: 'If you don't join there will
be a dispute situation.' That 'join or else' attitude, she claimed,
amounted to blackmail. She was later visited by Union officials at
different levels. 'It amounted to hectoring at the least and bullying
at the most', she said subsequently.

Mrs Kirk Smith decided against joining the Union and joined
the Institute instead. 'I do not approve of what the unions are
doing and I do not choose to be affiliated with the TUC', she said.
'The main issue is that I do not believe in closed shops for the
NUJ.'

The NUJ members at Darlington decided to strike over Mrs
Kirk Smith's employment and refusal to join the Union. The
strike was backed by the Union executive who saw it as an effort to
force the closed shop on Westminster Press. But they remained
adamant that a closed shop agreement would not be conceded.
They had negotiated harmoniously with both organisations, they
said. A free Press depended on the editor's power to determine
who should contribute to the paper, irrespective of whether the
contributors were members of the NUJ, IOJ or were non-union.

The dispute spread to the London offices of the group when three journalists were suspended for refusing to handle copy for any of the group's North of England newspapers and a number of their colleagues stopped work in sympathy over their suspension.

For nine weeks the papers were produced by editors and non-NUJ staff: then members of the National Graphical Association and the Society of Lithographic Artists, Designers, Engravers and Process Workers followed by members of the National Society of Operative Printers and Assistants, decided not to cross picket lines. As a result, the *Northern Echo* did not appear for the first time in its 107-year-old history. This was the paper which had been edited between 1871 and 1880 by the young social reformer, W. T. Stead, who rose to national stature, became editor of the *Pall Mall Gazette*, and contributed to the 'new journalism' of the 1890s with the invention of the big interview and the use of cross headings. His leading articles in the *Northern Echo* were quoted in Parliament and Gladstone once told him: 'To read the *Northern Echo* is to dispense with the necessity of reading other papers.'

One of the principal arguments in support of the closed shop has always been its value as a united front in securing improved pay and conditions. Yet, at Darlington, an offer by Westminster Press of a panel to review salaries to ensure they did not suffer through lack of a closed shop was rejected. It was apparent that the ideological claim for a closed shop was becoming an end in itself.

Towards the end of 1977 the strikers at Darlington were becoming increasingly isolated. The print unions returned to work, accusing the NUJ of intransigence, and the papers resumed publication. 'We have no intention of ending up with the situation where the NUJ have the closed shop at Darlington with no newspapers in which to operate it', said Mr Joe Wade, general secretary of the NGA.

Attempts to extend the strike to other Westminster Press offices met resistance and there was further isolation when the London staff returned to work.

The long and costly strike which had begun on 3 June ended on 10 January 1978. It had lasted seven months and cost an estimated £120 000 to the NUJ and £100 000 to the NGA. In addition, Westminster Press were reported to have lost more than

£1 million, to say nothing of the cost to newsprint suppliers and newsagents.

The attempt to make Darlington into a test case over the closed shop in journalism failed. The strikers decided to return to work on the basis of a face-saving formula which put the issue on ice, negotiated cash claims under the house agreement 'on the understanding', said Nicholas Herbert, the editorial director, 'that the NUJ have not obtained a closed shop, to which Westminster Press remains totally opposed'.

At Westminster, meanwhile, Mr Foot moved on to another appointment, leaving his successor, Mr Albert Booth, to grapple with the problem of the Press charter. The various parties, representing both sides of the industry, spent twelve months of long and patient effort thrashing out the arguments, but there were fundamental differences and it was apparent that consensus on a voluntary charter was impossible. The discussions ended in a series of pious clauses, supported in varying degree by the different parties, but without any agreement on the crucial question of the application of the closed shop to editorial departments.

The Institute had had little enthusiasm for the proposed charter from the time it was first suggested and provision made for it in the 1974 Act. It was felt that its purpose was purely cosmetic and that it could do nothing to restrict the undoubted freedom afforded by the Act to establish closed shops in journalism or to protect the employment of journalists who refused to join the closed shop union.

Mr Booth reported to Parliament that, following the industry's failure to agree on a voluntary charter, he would have discussions with the various parties before starting to draft a charter himself but before doing so he wanted to consider the report of the Royal Commission, which was then imminent.

When eventually it reported, the Royal Commission proposed six safeguards on Press freedom: that a journalist should have the freedom to speak and write without the threat of expulsion by an employer or union; that an editor should have the freedom to accept or reject any contribution, regardless of union membership or the author being a professional journalist; that an editor should be free to join a union or take part in industrial action if he or she chose; that the editor's right to accept or reject an article in spite of the views of management, a union or advertiser, should be protected; that a proper appeals procedure should be established for complaints of unfair or arbitrary expulsion or exclusion from a union; and that assurances should be obtained that practices of publishers, the NUJ, and IOJ in matters affecting journalists' freedom would conform with the spirit and provisions of the planned Press charter. It also came up with a totally unrealistic suggestion of yet another attempt to merge the two journalistic unions into one.

The summer months of 1977 were spent in ministerial interviews with different sections of the industry; they dragged on into the following year. The differences were so wide that the imposition of a charter would have exacerbated an already disagreeable situation. In any event, general election fever was already in the Westminster air and there was a feeling among Labour ministers that a public furore about the freedom of the Press would be unwise in that atmosphere. In any event Mr Booth must have known that in a period of minority Government he would never have been able to persuade the House of Commons to accept a charter that did not have within it a clause allowing a journalist to be free of union membership.

Mrs Margaret Thatcher was then leader of the Opposition and favourite to soon become Britain's first woman Prime Minister. It was thought useful and wise to invite her to dinner to hear of her intentions as regards the Press when she took up residence at 10 Downing Street.

Mrs Thatcher shared the Institute's scepticism of the value of the Press charter. Her comments on the dangers of a journalistic closed shop at that dinner in November 1978 are worth repeating:

The IOJ is to be congratulated on the robust stand it has taken against this proposal. Elements within the NUJ do wish to achieve a closed shop – so far, thank goodness, without success.

But is journalism just another industrial activity like mining or engineering? Surely not – journalism belongs to literature and to politics. Should there be a Writers' Union as there is in the Soviet Union? The idea should be abhorrent to us. Should there be a politicians' union to which all parliamentary candidates should belong? The idea is obnoxious to any democracy.

Why then should there be a union of writers and journalists with the sole right to issue a licence to print, and which would be the only body able to offer its members access to the public prints? The moderates in the NUJ say they seek a closed shop in order to raise pay. They see what the print unions are paid and, not unreasonably, they are jealous. But as you know there are extremists within the NUJ who would not only restrict access but also seek to control what their members might write.

The 'Trots' say that nothing should be written to offend the trades unions. They would discriminate against the National Front but not against the Socialist Workers' Party. And would there not be all kinds of dangers if all journalists were obliged to belong to the TUC, which is affiliated to the Labour movement?

A journalist whose function it is to express an opinion for public consumption would be placed more at risk by a closed shop than any other trade unionist. Newspapers exist not to protect their own freedom but to defend the freedom of others. Could a journalist succeed in doing that and still hold on to his licence?

In Britain we are seeing our freedoms chipped away one by one. A closed shop in journalism would mean handing over one of our most precious liberties to one union. Were the NUJ to consist entirely of saints it would not be right to give so much power to so few. The freedom of the Press underwrites all our other freedoms. If we remove it we shall all lose our liberty.

These then are my fears when I look at your profession from the outside. At present there is little that I can do to remove these dangers. If journalism is to be saved it will need the will and determination of journalists themselves.

When the General Election came a few months later the Conservative Party manifesto promised that further moves towards a closed shop in the newspaper industry would be resisted. The new Government's Employment Bill contained clauses that prevented some of the worst abuses of the closed shop in industry generally and extended the grounds on which dismissal might be unfair to embrace objections to union membership founded on 'conscience or other deeply held personal conviction'. This was specially appropriate in the case of journalists. But the Bill had limitations.

The Bill repealed the requirement to produce a Press charter and the Government subsequently produced a code of practice which strengthened to some extent the case of journalists. It created a conscience clause saying that a person could not be dismissed for non-membership of the union, made it more difficult to implement closed shops by reason of ballots and re-ballots, and provided for more generous compensation.

It was a disappointment that when first elected the Conservative Government did not outlaw entirely closed shops in journalism and that the manifesto for the succeeding election in 1983 made no promises at all on closed shops in the media.

While there are laws against discrimination in other areas, such as sex and race, there remains no protection for a person who wants to join a firm with a closed shop agreement with a union of which he or she is not a member.

This has disadvantaged IOJ members qualified and desirous of working in some of the most influential areas of the media, such as independent television and broadcasting. The BBC on the other hand refuses recognition to any union that will not undertake to refrain from seeking a closed shop.

13 Freedom of the Press

In carrying out the primary aim of the charter to promote by all reasonable means the interests of journalists and journalism, the Institute has faced change when the evolving techniques of the profession have demanded it, but one aspect that has remained paramount over the years is the maintenance and protection of freedom of the Press.

A series of loosely drawn laws have had an inhibiting effect on the Press: it has been hazardous in some instances for newspapers to comment or even report on a number of issues of public importance.

In the past few years, apart from three Royal Commissions on the Press, there have been a number of other official committees set up at the instigation of Government to examine various subjects which have a bearing on the working and freedoms of the Press.

Four such committees were in session at the beginning of the 1970s: the Franks Committee on the Official Secrets Act, the Phillimore Committee on Contempt; the Faulks Committee on defamation and the Younger Committee on privacy.

Contempt was the only one of the reports on which any real action was taken and even the new Act of 1981 so departed from the original recommendations that it caused concern and disappointment.

The record of lethargy in these matters by successive Governments carries the depressing inference that the importance of the Press is low in the order of priorities except, perhaps when it impinges directly on the Government or ministers themselves.

Writing in the Press Council's annual report for 1961–62 about incursions on Press freedom, Mr Cecil King, then chairman of the Mirror group of newspapers, thought that the Press was so hedged about by legal restrictions and penalties that it could no longer be called free. It was censored not directly or openly but by decree. He wrote:

The Official Secrets Acts are one of the chief forms of direct censorship: a high authority has remarked that the language of the Acts is wide enough to make it a criminal offence for a messenger in the Home Office to inform a journalist that the Permanent Under-Secretary is in the habit of taking six lumps of sugar in his tea. The law of libel is a nightmare: a territory full of pitfalls even for the most cautious, and the law of defamation remains a paradise for gold diggers. In the face of restrictions and oppressive penalties the voice of the British Press has grown timid.

Nevertheless there were journalists who were courageous in defending the hard-won rights of the Press: two members of the Institute were to figure in the courts for their actions – Brian Roberts, then Editor of the *Sunday Telegraph* and Harold Evans during his editorship of the *Sunday Times*. Both were recipients of the Institute's Gold Medal for their campaigns.

The gold medal was created in 1963 to be awarded to persons of whatever nationality, as occasion merited, in recognition of 'outstanding service to journalism and the fundamental freedom of the Press'. Its creation was the suggestion of one of the Institute's most respected and senior members, Mr H. J. Anthony French, who put the idea forward at the 1955 conference at Malvern.

All too often politicians and other public functionaries, who should be the principal defenders of a Free Press, are revealed as our most subtle and determined enemies. And the general public, who depend largely on journalists to sustain their own inherited freedoms, are either apathetic or indifferent or hostile until their individual rights are invaded – then, they cry to the Press to rescue them. On the other hand there are men and women of good will who in every civilised country have been sufficiently public-spirited to speak and act in our defence, and many besides journalists have been prepared to suffer for the freedom of the written word.

There have so far been six recipients, including Mr Roberts and Mr Evans. The first to receive the medal in 1964 was Mr Laurence Gandar, editor of the *Rand Daily Mail*, as a tribute to the 'unflinching courage with which he fought persistent attempts of the South African Government to curb the freedom of the anti-apartheid press'; in 1966 Dr Ahmed Emin Yalman, president of the Turkish Press Institute and editor of *Vatan*, received it for his unrelenting insistence for more than fifty years, despite exile, imprisonment and attempted assassination, on the rights of the Press to publish all points of view, however unacceptable to authority; Mrs Helen Vlachos, the Greek newspaper owner, was awarded the medal in 1968 for her courageous fight for newspaper freedom in Greece where, by refusing to publish in conditions of Press censorship under the junta, she made Press freedom a first principle; and in 1970 it was awarded to M. Hubert Beuve-Mery, founder and for twenty-five years editor of *Le Monde*, for outstanding services to Press freedom through his newspaper which, under his direction, not only achieved the highest standards of independence but also won an unrivalled position as a newspaper of merit.

Mr Brian Roberts, a past President of the Institute, had risked prosecution in the interests of Press freedom by challenging the iniquity of Section 2 of the Official Secrets Act in publishing a confidential report about the Nigerian conflict. That section of the Act had been an irritant to the Institute and others since its introduction in 1906.

Mr Roberts and his co-defendants were acquitted after a trial lasting twenty-two days at the Old Bailey. His testimony from the witness box was so eloquent and compelling that it not only convinced the jury that he should be acquitted but it brought from the Judge, Mr Justice Caulfield, a call for the Act to be reformed.

The Judge presented in a nutshell the Institute's entire case. In his summing up, he said that if it did nothing else the case might alert those who governed us to consider whether Section 2 had reached retirement age and should be pensioned off. Everyone realised that the Press must not be muzzled. Then, in a subsequently well-quoted phrase, he put the kernel of the whole matter: 'Its warning bark is necessary to help maintain a free society. If the Press is the watchdog of freedom and its fangs are drawn all that will ensue is a whimper – not a bark.'

Apart from its wider significance, the ending of the trial afforded a unique Institute occasion. The reigning President, George Glenton who, as a crime reporter, has the Old Bailey as his base, was able to step into the dock to congratulate Mr Roberts on his acquittal on behalf of the Institute and every other journalist in the land: the only occasion on which past and present presidents of the Institute have shaken hands on the spot where so many infamous criminals have stood. Some months later Mr Glenton presided over the ceremony at which Mr Roberts was presented with his rare award.

It was generally conceded that the *Sunday Telegraph* prosecution had been a mistake and in evidence to the Franks Committee the Institute, along with others, submitted that Section 2 was unnecessary and should be abolished and not replaced. When the Committee reported in September 1972, it proposed that Section 2 of the Act should be repealed and replaced by a new statute called the Official Information Act which should apply to defence matters and foreign relations. After such displays of strong opposition to the infamous section, it is astonishing that over a decade later it should still remain in existence on the Statute Book.

Mr Harold Evans, the last recipient of the gold medal in 1980, made an international reputation as a campaigning journalist and editor in the best traditions of his predecessor as editor of the *Northern Echo*, W. T. Stead. Evans conducted his campaigns in the *Sunday Times*, of which he was editor for fourteen years from 1967, after leaving the *Echo*.

His most notable campaign on behalf of thalidomide children developed into a fight against legal restrictions on a newspaper's right to freedom of expression. It began in September 1972 when the *Sunday Times* printed its first article about thalidomide children which it intended to follow up with a history of the tragedy and the manufacture and testing of the drug in 1958–61. The manufacturers of the drug, Distillers Co. (Biochemicals) Ltd, made formal representations to the Attorney-General claiming that the article constituted contempt of court because of litigation that was still outstanding. The Attorney-General decided to apply to the High Court for an injunction to restrain publication of the proposed article, which was granted. Times Newspapers then succeeded in getting the decision reversed by the Court of Appeal. But on a further appeal by the Attorney-General to the House of Lords, the Law Lords unanimously confirmed the original finding that the proposed article sought to interfere with pending court proceedings, including settlement negotiations between claimants and Distillers, and therefore constituted contempt.

The tenacious Evans refused to give up and the case was

referred to the European Commission of Human Rights in Strasburg. It was the first case to be submitted to the Commission by a British newspaper. Evans claimed that the court order preventing publication of an article was a violation of Article 10 of the European Convention on Human Rights. This article states:

> If the public interest to clarify matters of great importance cannot be satisfied by any kind of official investigation, it must, in a democratic society, at least be allowed to find expression in another way. Only the most pressing grounds can be sufficient to justify that the authorities stop information on matters, the clarification of which would seem to lie in the public interest.

The Commission ruled by eight votes to five in his favour and the case went on to a full trial in the Court of Human Rights. The oral arguments were heard in April 1978 and a year later the court found there had been a violation of Article 10.

It brought about a redefinition of the English law: an Act in 1982 changed the starting point of *sub judice* from the issuing of a writ to the later time when a case is set down for trial.

14 The Future

A new threat to the traditional local Press has emerged in the last decade or so with the widespread introduction of free newspapers – advertising sheets in the main with a minimum of local news, delivered to every household in an area.

This type of free newspaper is not a new phenomenon: before the Second World War there were many such papers, some of which were converted to traditional local newspapers when war was declared in order to qualify for an allocation of newsprint. What is new is their rapid growth and their displacement in many homes of the paid-for local newspaper.

A new branch of the industry has grown, menacing old established local papers which have been affected by diminished sales and advertising revenue. Local newspapers still sell over 9 million copies a week, but their circulations have suffered a severe decline of 2.5 million over a decade. At the same time, the weekly circulation of free newssheets has risen to 24 million and they are absorbing 20 per cent of the advertising placed with provincial newspapers. Some established newspaper groups have added free newspapers to their publications either to gain a foothold on the new bandwagon or, in some instances, to stifle the opposition.

Free newspapers have become the fastest growing media form in Britain and one increasingly accepted by major advertisers. Before their advent, the traditional local newspaper had enjoyed a monopoly: the entrepreneurs of the free newspaper disturbed the mood of lethargy into which the regional newspapers had sunk.

This was the theme of Mr Ian Fletcher, chairman of the Association of Free Newspapers, at its third annual conference in 1983 when he predicted change afoot throughout the whole regional press.

The major groups are moving more decisively than ever into the field of free publishing and whilst in many cases they have not ironed out all their problems their newspapers are serious contenders for major markets.

Now practically every urban centre in the UK is provided with choice for the advertiser, which must in itself be symbolic of a healthy democracy. So we seem to be facing a repeat of the rationalisation of twenty years ago but this time brought about by the competition introduced by free newspapers. We all, paid or free, are within the broad banner of the regional newspaper publishing industry. Sadly, however, there would appear to be ever increasing efforts to isolate independent free publishers who have proved to be the lifeblood of the industry and we could now unfortunately be approaching the stage of confrontation or co-operation.

The local newspaper in many instances has undergone change in its appearance in meeting its opposition. The traditional local weekly newspaper fare of reports of the doings of its local organisations and people has frequently been displaced by the introduction of more feature material, such as film and television reviews, notwithstanding that these are available in the national and regional newspapers by writers of greater authority. Many local papers have also been bitten by the investigative journalism bug of their national contemporaries. Campaigning journalism, however, is more difficult to maintain in the confines of a local circulation area. While the growth of local authorities and other public bodies has strengthened the need for vigilance by local newspapers in protecting the public interest, there is a danger that, unless practised carefully and dispassionately, relatively innocuous matters can be exaggerated in the pursuit of maladministration.

As the IOJ moves into another century, the British newspaper industry is on the threshold of a revolution which has already been met and mastered elsewhere in the world: the revolution of new technology.

The Institute is the only union in British newspaper publishing that has consistently advocated the full exploitation of modern technology. Journalists are the initiators of newspaper content: it is logical that they should input their material into the computerised process direct.

From experience elsewhere the advantages of the new methods are seen in the speeding up of systems of communication and production, with greater profitability resulting when the opportunities are fully exploited.

In Britain, what progress has been made on the introduction of new technologies has been mainly in the provincial press. In Fleet Street various schemes have been planned by different newspaper offices but union opposition has virtually kept the brakes firmly on the introduction of new systems, even despite warnings from some print union leaders of its inevitability.

The Institute, through its technology committee, played a prominent part in 1982 in the Government-sponsored Information Technology Year. Since then, the Minister for Information Technology, Mr Kenneth Baker, among others, has warned of the newspaper industry's urgent need to embrace the technological advance: in a phrase, to modernise or fossilise. He told the Newspaper Society in April 1984:

> Newspapers represent one of the first industries based on information. The technology used by many newspapers has changed only a little since the early 1950s, in spite of major technological advances in information processing. Modern computer typesetting and word processing equipment allows the rapid manipulation of information yet it is the minority of newspapers, particularly in Fleet Street, which have been able to benefit fully from this technology. . . . We are seeing our newspaper industry simply unable to grasp the opportunities which new technology opens up. While local newspapers have been able to adopt new technology on a wider scale, Fleet Street has remained embedded in another age. . . .
>
> New technology can allow newspapers to compete better with the new electronic information services. Having up-to-date news, a more efficient classified advertising service, and the ability to produce more pages more cheaply, there is a good chance of our newspapers seeing rising circulations once more and increased advertising revenue. At the very worst, if newspapers do not adopt the new technologies, they will simply and slowly disappear just as the dinosaurs disappeared into the alluvial slime. . . . The march of new technology is inexorable. What you have to decide is whether you are going to march with it or be trampled under foot.

Throughout the history of journalism for most of the present century, as shown in these pages, there has existed a conflict on the status of the profession. That conflict, between those journalists who maintain a justified pride in their calling as a profession and seek to improve its status and those who seek to improve the conditions and benefits through traditional trade union methods shows no sign of solution as we approach the next century.

The weight of trade union activity in which the organisation is increasingly forced to take part is an inevitable progression of its role which need not diminish its established position as a professional body. The two aspects do not militate against each other: indeed they are often synonymous and can be mutually beneficial. The trade union activities of the Institute, performed as they are in a responsible manner, give credence and stature to the organisation which reflects on its professional activities. The reverse is also true.

Four attempts to bring about a unified organisation have failed. The very diversity of journalists and journalism is a barrier to unity and in the maintenance of the freedom of the Press in general terms and the freedom of choice of individual journalists, it is essential to have a strong alternative to safeguard and protect, among other things, the position of journalists who, for whatever reason, may find their ability to work jeopardised or who hold firm convictions against joining a trade union which pursues political aims or has strong political attachments.

The IOJ is by modern standards one of the smaller unions, but it is far from insignificant. History has shown that, given goodwill, there can be not only co-existence between the two journalistic organisations but co-operation in the achievement of mutual aims.

That is a theme which could with profit also be practised elsewhere in the newspaper industry. There is an urgent need for the future survival of an ancient and honourable industry to halt the treadmill of distrust and confrontation which has bedevilled it for too long and to step onto the firmer ground of friendlier co-operation – between different unions and between unions and managements – so that all engaged in it may reap the benefits and rewards that are available.

Appendix 1: The Royal Charter

VICTORIA, BY THE GRACE OF GOD, of the United Kingdom of Great Britain and Ireland, Queen Defender of the Faith; TO ALL TO whom these Presents shall come, Greeting;

WHEREAS certain of Our subjects Members of an Association or Society formerly known as 'The National Association of Journalists', and now known as 'The Institute of Journalists', whose names are hereinafter set forth have petitioned Us for a Charter of Incorporation such as is in hand by these Presents granted.

AND whereas We are minded to comply with the prayer of such petitition.

NOW therefore We of Our especial grace certain knowledge and mere motion Do hereby for Us Our Heirs and Successors will grant direct appoint and declare as follows:

1. HUGH GILZEAN REID, of Warley Hall, Worcestershire, Journalist; SIR ALGERNON BORTHWICK, Baronet, Member of Parliament, of 139, Piccadilly, London, Journalist; EDWARD LAWSON, of Hall Barn, Beaconsfield, Buckinghamshire, Journalist; SIR EDWIN ARNOLD, Knight, Master of Arts, of 21, West Cromwell Road, Kensington, Middlesex, Journalist; JUSTIN MACCARTHY, Member of Parliament, of 20, Cheyne Gardens, Chelsea, Middlesex, Journalist; JAMES MACKENZIE MACLEAN, Member of Parliament, of 40, Nevern Square, Earl's Court, Middlesex, Journalist; PETER WILLIAM CLAYDEN, of 13, Tavistock Square, London, Journalist; HARRY FURNISS, of 23, St. Edmund's Terrace, Regent's Park, London, Journalist; EDWARD RICHARD RUSSELL, of Liverpool, Journalist; JOHN ARCHIBALD WILLOX, of Liverpool, Journalist; THOMAS SOWLER, Colonel, of Manchester, Journalist; HENRY FLINT, of Manchester, Journalist; JOHN THACKRAY BUNCE, of Birmingham, Journalist; JAMES ANNAND, of Newcastle-on-Tyne, Journalist; WILLIAM DUNCAN, of Newcastle-on-Tyne, Journalist; ROBERT EADON LEADER, Bachelor of Arts, of Sheffield, Journalist; CHARLES CLIFFORD, of Sheffield, Journalist; ALBERT GROSER, of Plymouth, Journalist; THOMAS DAVID TAYLOR, of Bristol, Journalist; ROBERT JONES GRIFFITHS, Master of Arts and Doctor of Laws, of 4, Middle Temple Lane, London, Journalist; CHARLES RUSSELL, of Glasgow, Journalist; RICHARD GOWING, of Upper Park Road, Hampstead, Middlesex, Journalist; EDWARD EDEN PEACOCK, of 5, Tierney Road, Streatham Hill, Surrey, Journalist; BENJAMIN DAIN HOPGOOD, of 4, Westwick Gardens, West Kensington Park, London, Journalist; HERBERT SAMUEL CORNISH, of 80, Victoria Road, Stroud Green, Middlesex, Journalist and Secretary; and such other persons as now are members of the said Society known as the 'Institute of Journalists', and all such

persons as may hereafter become members of the Body Corporate hereby constituted according to the Provisions of these Presents and their Successors shall for ever hereafter be by virtue of these Presents, one body politic and corporate by the name of 'The Institute of Journalists', and by the name aforesaid, shall have perpetual succession and a Common Seal, with full power and authority to alter, vary, break and renew the same at their discretion and by the same name to sue and be sued, implead and be impleaded, answer and be answered unto, in every court of Us, Our Heirs and Successors; and shall be able and capable in law to take, purchase and hold to them and their successors notwithstanding the Statutes of Mortmain, any lands, tenements or hereditaments whatsoever situated within Our United Kingdom of Great Britain and Ireland, not exceeding in the whole the annual value of £3,000, such annual value to be circulated and ascertained at the respective periods or times of acquiring the same: And shall be able and capable in law to grant, demise, alien or otherwise dispose the lands, tenements or hereditaments belonging to the Institute of Journalists and also to do all other matters incidental or appertaining to a body corporate.

2. THE objects and purposes for which the Institute of Journalists (hereinafter and in the Schedule to these Presents called 'the Institute') is hereby constituted are the following:

(a) Devising measures for testing the qualifications of candidates for admission to professional membership of the Institute by examination in theory and in practice or by any other actual and practical tests;

(b) The promotion of whatever may tend to the elevation of the status and the improvement of the qualifications of all Members of the Journalistic profession;

(c) The ascertainment of the law and practice relating to all things connected with the Journalistic profession and the exercise of supervision over its Members when engaged in professional duties;

(d) The collection, collation and publication of information of service or interest to Members of the Journalistic profession;

(e) Watching any legislation affecting the discharge by Journalists of their professional duties and endeavouring to obtain amendments of the law affecting Journalists, their duties or interests;

(f) Acting as a means of communication between Members or others seeking professional engagements and employers desirous of employing them;

(g) Promoting personal and friendly intercourse between Members of the Institute; holding conferences and meetings for the discussion of professional affairs, interests and duties; the compilation, constant revision and publication of lists and registers of Journalists and of records of events and proceedings of interest to Journalists;

(h) The formation of a library for the use of Members of the Institute;

(i) The encouragement, establishment or development of a professional journal for Journalists;

(j) The promotion, encouragement or assistance of means for providing against the exigencies of age, sickness, death and misfortune;

(k) The acquisition by the Institute of a hall or other permanent place of meeting and of other places of meeting;

(l) Securing the advancement of Journalism in all its branches and obtaining for Journalists as such formal and definite professional standing;

(m) The promotion by all reasonable means of interests of Journalists and Journalism.

3. THE Institute shall not carry on any trade or business or engage in any transactions with a view to the pecuniary profit or gain of the members thereof, and the members of the Institute shall not seek or derive any pecuniary profit or gain from the Institute or their membership thereof.

4. THE Institute shall consist of a President, Vice-Presidents (not exceeding 15 in number), a Council (not exceeding 60 in number), and such classes of Members as may be from time to time prescribed by Bye-laws of the Institute. The President and Vice-Presidents shall, *ex officio*, be Members of the Council.

5. THE first President shall be the said Hugh Gilzean Reid, the first Vice-Presidents shall be the said Sir Algernon Borthwick, the said Edward Lawson, the said Peter William Clayden, the said Thomas David Taylor, the said Charles Russell, the said John Archibald Willox, the said Benjamin Dain Hopgood, the said William Duncan, Henry John Palmer, of Birmingham, Journalist, John Wilson, of Edinburgh, Journalist, and John Vaughan of Leicester, Journalist; the first Members of the Council shall be the said President and Vice-Presidents, and the said Edward Eden Peacock and the said Charles Clifford.

The said President, Vice-Presidents and Members of the Council shall hold office until the due election of their successors in accordance with the Bye-laws of the Institute.

6. THE Institute shall have such permanent officers as the Bye-laws of the Institute may prescribe and such other Officers and Servants as the Council may from time to time appoint.

7. THE government of the Institute and its affairs shall be vested in the Council. The Council shall obey the directions of these Presents and the Bye-laws of the Institute.

8. THE Council shall have power from time to time to make Bye-laws of the Institute and from time to time to revoke, alter or amend any Bye-laws thertofore made. **Provided** that no such Bye-laws or any such revocation, alteration or amendment shall take effect until the same have or has been submitted to and sanctioned by a General Meeting of the Institute with respect to which due notice has been given that such new Bye-laws or such revocation, alteration or amendment will be taken in consideration at such General Meeting.

9. THE Bye-laws of the Institute may provide with respect to all or any of the following matters:

(i) The carrying out of any of the objects of the Institute;

(ii) The qualifications, election, amotion and classification of members of the Institute and the conditions of Membership (including contributions to the funds of the Institute);

(iii) The qualifications, election, amotion, continuance in office and duties of the President, Vice-Presidents and Members of the Council and the number of Vice-Presidents and Members of the Council;

(iv) The qualifications, appointment, dismissal, duties and remuneration of the Officers and Servants of the Institute;

(v) The summoning, holding and proceedings of General Meetings (including the voting at such meetings and the rights and duties of Members present thereat and the quorum necessary to constitute the same);

(vi) The summoning, holding and proceedings of Meetings of the Council; the quorum of the Council and the business powers and duties of the Council;

(vii) The appointment of Committees of the Council or Institute for inquiring and reporting to either the Council or General Meetings or for the management of any part of the affairs of the Institute or the promotion or execution of any of its objects;

(viii) The management of the funds and property of the Institute and the conduct of the business of the Institute;

(ix) The organisation of the Institute by the division of the United Kingdom or any parts thereof into Districts and the appointment of District Committees of the Institute and District Officers and the qualifications, election, amotion, continuance in office of the members of such Committees, and the qualifications and tenure of such Officers and the powers and duties of such Committees and Officers;

(x) Any matters connected with or relating to any of the matters aforesaid;

(xi) Any matters connected with or relating to the affairs or government of the Institute.

Provided Always that the said Bye-laws shall comply with the provisions and directions of these Presents and shall not be in any manner repugnant thereto or to the laws and statutes of this Realm and **Provided** also that the said Bye-laws and any revocation, alteration, or amendment thereof shall not be of any force or effect until the same shall have been allowed by the Lords of Our Privy Council of which allowance a Certificate under the hand of the Clerk of Our Privy Council shall be conclusive evidence.

10. THE first Bye-laws to be made under these Presents shall be made and sanctioned by a General Meeting of the Institute within the space of two years from the date hereof unless the Lords of Our Privy Council shall see fit to extend such period of which extension the Certificate of the Clerk of Our Privy Council shall be conclusive evidence.

11. PENDING the making, sanction and allowance of Bye-laws to be made

under these Presents but no longer the Bye-laws in the Schedule to the Presents set forth shall be the Bye-laws of the Institute and observed as such.

12. THE Council of the Institute shall be at liberty at any time or times hereafter to apply to Us Our Heirs and Successors for a supplementary Charter or Charters and such Charter or Charters when accepted in such manner and by such proportion and such of the Members of the Institute as shall in such Charter or Charters be provided in that behalf shall be binding upon the Institute and all the Members thereof and to all other intents and purposes whatsoever and shall repeal so much of these Presents or any Supplementary Charter as shall be inconsistent therewith and these Presents and all such Supplementary Charters shall be construed as one instrument.

13. AND **we do hereby** for Us Our Heirs and Successors, **Grant and Declare,** that these Our Letters Patent shall be in all things good, firm, valid and effectual in the law according to the true intent and meaning of the same and shall be taken, construed and adjudged, in all our Courts and elsewhere, in the most favourable and beneficial sense and for the best advantage of the said Institute of Journalists, any misrecital, non-recital, omission, defect, imperfection, matter or thing whatsoever notwithstanding:

In WITNESS whereof we have caused these Our Letters to be made Patent WITNESS Ourself at Westminster, the third day of March, in the fifty-third year of Our reign.

THE SCHEDULE above referred to being the **Provisional Bye-laws of the Institute of Journalists.** (Here followed in the Charter the Provisional Bye-laws, since replaced by other Bye-laws.)

BY WARRANT UNDER THE QUEEN'S SIGN MANUAL

MUIR MACKENZIE.

Supplemental Charter

ELIZABETH THE SECOND BY THE GRACE OF GOD of the United Kingdom of Great Britain and Northern Ireland and of Our other Realms and Territories Queen, Head of the Commonwealth, Defender of the Faith: TO ALL TO whom these Presents shall come, Greeting!

WHEREAS Her Majesty Queen Victoria in the year of our Lord One thousand eight hundred and ninety by Royal Charter dated the third day of March in the fifty-third year of Her Reign (hereinafter referred to as 'the Charter') constituted a body corporate and politic by the name of 'The Institute of Journalists' (hereinafter referred to as 'the Institute'):

AND WHEREAS it has been represented unto Us that it is expedient that the objects and purposes of the Institute should be extended and that Article 12 of the Charter should be revoked:

AND WHEREAS supplication has been made unto Us to grant to the Institute a Supplemental Charter for the above-mentioned purposes:

NOW THEREFORE KNOW YE that We, by virtue of Our prerogative Royal and of all other powers enabling Us in that behalf have, of Our especial grace, and mere motion granted and declared and by these Presents do grant and declare notwithstanding anything to the contrary contained in the Charter, as follows:

1. ARTICLE 12 of the Charter is hereby revoked.

2. THE objects and purposes of the Institute shall notwithstanding anything contained in the Charter and in addition to the objects and purposes therein specified henceforth include the promotion of a Bill or Bills in Parliament for securing the amalgamation of the Institute with the registered trade union now known as the National Union of Journalists or with any other body corporate, association or other combination whatsoever whose objects are conducive to the furtherance of the interests of Journalists and Journalism if such amalgamation shall be for the advancement of Journalism. The Institute may promote such a Bill or Bills either alone or in conjunction with the said trade union or such other body corporate, association or combination as aforesaid.

3. ALL the provisions of the Charter and of this Our Supplemental Charter shall be revoked as from the date on which any such amalgamation secured as aforesaid takes effect.

IN WITNESS whereof We have caused these Our Letters to be made Patent.

WITNESS Ourself at Westminster the 28th day of January in the nineteenth year of Our Reign.

BY WARRANT UNDER THE QUEEN'S SIGN MANUAL

W. G. AGNEW.

Supplemental Charter

ELIZABETH THE SECOND BY THE GRACE OF GOD of the United Kingdom of Great Britain and Northern Ireland and of Our other Realms and Territories Queen, Head of the Commonwealth, Defender of the Faith: TO ALL TO WHOM THESE PRESENTS SHALL COME, GREETING!

WHEREAS Her Majesty Queen Victoria in the year of our Lord One thousand eight hundred and ninety by Royal Charter dated the third day of March in the fifty-third year of Her Reign (hereinafter referred to as 'the Charter') constituted a body corporate and politic by the name of 'The Institute of Journalists' (hereinafter referred to as 'the Institute'):

AND WHEREAS in the year One thousand nine hundred and seventy-one by Letters Patent dated the twenty-eighth day of January in the nineteenth year of Our Reign We were graciously pleased to grant to the Institute a Supplemental Charter (hereinafter referred to as 'the Supplemental Charter') by which the objects and purposes of the Institute were extended and Article 12 of the Charter revoked:

AND WHEREAS it has been represented unto Us that it is expedient that certain provisions of the Supplemental Charter should be revoked:

AND WHEREAS supplication has been made unto Us to grant the Institute a further Supplemental Charter for the above-mentioned purpose:

NOW THEREFORE KNOW YE that We, by virtue of Our Prerogative Royal and of all other powers enabling Us in that behalf of Our especial grace, certain knowledge and mere motion granted and declared and by these Presents do for Us, Our Heirs and Successors grant and declare notwithstanding anything to the contrary contained in the Charter or Supplemental Charter that all the provisions of the Supplemental Charter save that of Article 1 thereof (whereby Article 12 of the Charter was revoked) shall be and the same are hereby revoked.

IN WITNESS whereof We have caused these Our Letters to be made Patent.

WITNESS Ourself at Westminster the thirteenth day of October in the twenty-fourth year of Our Reign.

BY WARRANT UNDER THE QUEEN'S SIGN MANUAL

N. E. LEIGH.

Appendix 2: A Parade of Presidents

Some of the greatest names in journalism have distinguished the Roll of Honour of Past Presidents of the Institute of Journalists. The men (and one woman) who have led the Institute have come from many parts of the British Isles and represent every branch of the profession.

1883–86	Harry Flint (Manchester)
1886–88	Lord Glenesk (London)
1888–90	Sir Hugh Gilzean Reid (London)
1890–91	Lord Glenesk (London)
1891–92	Lord Burnham (London)
1892–93	Charles Russell (Glasgow)
1893–94	P. W. Clayden (London)
1894–95	Thomas Crosbie (Cork)
1895–96	Sir John A. Willox (Liverpool)
1896–97	J. M. Maclean (Cardiff)
1897–98	Lord Russell (Liverpool)
1898–99	Sir Wemyss Reid (London)
1899–1900	Sir James Henderson (Belfast)
1900–01	Arthur W. A'Beckett (London)
1901–02	Henry J. Palmer (Leeds)
1902–03	Alexander W. Still (Birmingham)
1903–04	J. Nicol Dunn (London)
1904–05	David T. Sanderman (Glasgow)
1905–06	Major George F. Gratwicke (Exeter)
1906–07	Sir Frederick W. Wilson (Ipswich)
1907–08	Sir Alfred F. Robbins (London)
1908	J. E. Woolacott (London)
1908–09	Samuel S. Campion (Northampton)
1909–10	Viscount Burnham CH (London)
1910–11	John Mitchell (Dundee)
1911–12	George B. Hodgson (South Shields)
1913	Sir Robert Donald (London)
1914	James Sykes (Leeds)
1915–16	Alfred G. Gardiner (London)
1917–18	J. L. Garvin (London)
1919	F. Hinde (London)
1920–21	George Springfield (London)

1922	Charles Wells (Bristol)
1923–25	Frederick Peaker (London)
1926	Sir Robert Bruce (Glasgow)
1927	Sir Charles Igglesden (Kent)
1928	Ralph D. Blumenfeld (London)
1929–30	H. A. Gwynne (London)
1931	William Charles Chillingworth (Dublin)
1932–33	Sir Emsley Carr (London)
1934	Henry J. Whittick (Wolverhampton)
1935	Alan Pitt Robbins (London)
1936–37	Hugh W. Dawson (Edinburgh)
1938	H. A. Taylor (London)
1939	John Sayers (Ulster)
1940	P. E. Verstone (London)

Hon. Charter President:
J. A. Spender CH

1941	W. R. Willis (Yorkshire)
1942–43	Gordon Robbins (London)
1944	William Redfern (North-Eastern)
1945	Harold Ffoulkes (London)
1946	W. Linton Andrews (Yorkshire)
1947	A. T. Penman (London)
1948	J. Murray Watson (Edinburgh)
1949	John Gordon (London)
1950	F. K. Gardiner (Sheffield)
1951	Norman Robson (London)
1951–52	Arthur B. Hunt (Sussex)
1952–53	A. J. Cummings (London)
1953–54	Douglas C. Stephen (South Wales)
1954–55	Brian R. Roberts (London)
1955–56	Alexander Boath (Belfast)
1956–57	Reginald M. Lester (London)
1957–58	H. Roy Wiltshire (Wolverhampton)
1958–59	Herbert Gunn (London)
1959–60	Lewis Simpson (Edinburgh)
1960–61	S. R. Pawley (London)
1961–62	Alan H. Simpson (York)
1962–63	H. H. Hayman (London)
1963–64	William Rees-Mogg (London)
1965	S. Morley Tonkin (Shropshire and Mid-Wales)
1966	D. C. Flatley (Essex)
1967–68	Miss M. D. Peacocke (London)
1968–69	Keith Gascoigne (Birmingham)
1969–70	A. Norman Walker (London)
1970–71	Eric J. Barker (Cumberland and Westmorland)
1971–72	George Glenton (London)
1972–73	Henry R. Douglas (London)
1973–74	James Mather (London)

1974–75	Cynric Mytton-Davies (Freelance)
1975–76	George Withy (Liverpool)
1976–77	Maurice Green (London)
1977–78	John Slim (Birmingham)
1978–79	Cyril Bainbridge (Fleet Street)
1979–80	Walter McVitie (Freelance)
1980–81	Christopher Underwood (Broadcasting)
1981–82	Graham Jones (Home Counties)
1982–83	William D. Tadd (Fleet Street)
1983–84	Kenneth J. Brookes (Freelance)
1984–85	Barrie Farnhill (Yorkshire)

Appendix 3: General Secretaries

The Institute of Journalists has been fortunate in having only four general secretaries throughout its history.

1886–1926	Herbert S. Cornish
1926–36	R. V. Walling
1936–62	Stewart Nicholson
1962–	Robert F. Farmer

Index